Charles Stuart Calverley

Translations into English and Latin

Charles Stuart Calverley

Translations into English and Latin

ISBN/EAN: 9783337185497

Printed in Europe, USA, Canada, Australia, Japan

Cover: Foto ©Paul-Georg Meister /pixelio.de

More available books at **www.hansebooks.com**

CHARLES STUART CALVERLEY
TRANSLATIONS
INTO ENGLISH AND LATIN

LONDON: GEORGE BELL AND SONS
CAMBRIDGE: DEIGHTON BELL AND CO.
MDCCCXCVII

First edition, 1866.
Reprinted 1885.
Cheaper edition, 1896.
Reprinted 1897.

PREFACE.

OF the following Translations, those into Latin were done for pupils at College, and a few, both of them and of the English ones, have been in print before. As they were mixed up with verses of a lighter kind, and probably did not come under the notice of most of those who will read the present volume, they have been reprinted here. On one (Horace, Book I. Ode 11) a reviewer observed that the last line was "a reminiscence of the Princess," as of course it was. To anticipate any similar criticisms it may be worth while to say a few words.

I have nowhere adopted a phrase or word of any previous translator. I had translated the first Iliad before Lord Derby's or Mr. Wright's Homer appeared, and the second before I had seen their versions. The same remark applies, *mutatis mutandis*, to Professor Conington's Horace. I did not know till I had finished the Eclogues that any translation of them existed, for Dryden's, I suppose, scarcely counts as a translation. Since then I have met with Mr. Kennedy's Virgil, and availed myself of it to correct my rendering of line 79 of Eclogue III.

On the other hand, I have taken without scruple any expression of an original writer which seemed to me to be the equivalent of the Latin or Greek with which I had to deal. And as I happen to have borrowed in all cases from well-known writers, and passages which must be familiar to every one who reads at all, I have not thought it necessary to call attention to the fact each time, by quotation commas or otherwise. Quotation commas for this purpose are, I think, open to more objections than one: and surely it would be superfluous to specify in a note that *e.g.* such a phrase as " catch the blossom of to-day " was caught from Tennyson.

C. S. C.

CONTENTS.

TRANSLATIONS INTO ENGLISH.

		PAGE
Homer, Iliad I.		1
,, ,, II.		30
,, ,, I. In Hexameters		70
Virgil, Eclogue I.		81
,, ,, II.		87
,, ,, III.		91
,, ,, IV.		97
,, ,, V.		100
,, ,, VI.		105
,, ,, VII.		109
,, ,, VIII.		113
,, ,, IX.		119
,, ,, X.		122
Horace's Odes, Bk. I. Ode 9.	To Thaliarchus	127
,, ,, ,, 11.	To Leuconoë	130
,, ,, ,, 14.	To a Ship	131
,, ,, ,, 24.	To Virgil	132
,, ,, ,, 28.	To Archytas	134
,, ,, ,, 38.	To his Slave	138
,, ,, Bk. III. 1.	Odi profanum	137
,, ,, ,, 2.	Angustam, amice	139
,, ,, ,, 3.	Justum et tenacem	141
,, ,, ,, 4.	Descende cœlo	144
,, ,, ,, 5.	Cœlo tonantem	148
,, ,, ,, 6.	Delicta majorum	151

CONTENTS.

	PAGE
HORACE's ODES, Bk. III. 13. To the Fount of Bandusia	153
„ „ „ 18. To a Faun	154
„ „ Bk. IV. 13. To Lyce	156
HORACE, Epode 2. Beatus ille	157
From VIRGIL, Georgic, iii. 515	161
„ SOPHOCLES, Ajax, 645	162
„ LUCRETIUS, Bk. II.	164
„ CATULLUS, Sirmio	170

TRANSLATIONS INTO LATIN.

Lycidas (*Milton*)	171
Boadicea (*Cowper*)	188
Come live with me. (*Marlowe*)	192
If all the world (*Raleigh*)	194
While musing thus (*Bradstreet*)	196
Sweet day (*Herbert*)	198
In memoriam (*Tennyson*)	200
Tears, idle tears (*Tennyson*)	202
Ps. lv. verses 4—8	204
Of holier joy (*Trench*)	206
From the Analogy (*Butler*)	208
Fountain that sparklest	210
Go up and watch (*Keble*)	210
Winter (*Thomson*)	214
Leaves have their time (*Hemans*)	216
My Brother's Grave (*Moultrie*)	218
Let us turn (*Trench*)	220
Œnone (*Tennyson*)	222
The Soldier's Dream (*Campbell*)	224
From the Giaour (*Byron*)	226
Gleniffer (*Tannahill*)	228
He sung what spirit (*Cowley*)	230

CONTENTS.

	PAGE
The Nereid maids (*Landor*)	232
Weep no more (*Fletcher*)	234
Glumdalclitch's Lament (*Pope*)	236
Laura Matilda's Dirge (*Rejected Addresses*)	238
Herrick Amarillis (*Herrick*)	242
Ca' the Ewes (*Burns*)	244
The Gentle Shepherd (*Ramsay*)	246
Poor Tree (*Carlisle*)	248
XLIV. Christmas	252
CXXX. Pentecost	253
CXXXIX.	254
CXCVII.	255
CCXX.	257
CCXLII. Dedication of a Church	258

HOMER'S ILIAD. BOOK I.

THE wrath of Peleus' son, that evil wrath
   Which on Achaia piled a myriad woes,
Oh Goddess, sing: which down to darkness hurled
Brave souls of mighty men, and made their flesh
A prey to dogs and every ravening fowl.   5
Yet Zeus his will was working: since the day
When first 'twixt Atreus' son, the King of men,
And proud Achilles there arose up war.

   What god, then, bade those twain stand forth
      and strive?
Zeus's and Leto's son.   He, angered sore   10
Against the King, sent pestilence abroad
Among the army, that the people died:
For that of Atreus' son had been disdained
His servant, Chryses.   To redeem his child
With ransom measureless had Chryses come   15

Ev'n to the Achaian war-ships—in his hand
The emblem of the god who smites from far,
Apollo, high upon a staff of gold.
To all the Greeks he prayed, but most of all
To Atreus' sons, twin captains of the host. 20

"O Atreus' sons, and bravely-harnessed Greeks!
The gods, whose dwelling is Olympus, grant
That ye may sack Priam's city, and regain
Your homes rejoicing! Yea and unto me
May give my child, my own, and take her price, 25
Since great is Zeus's son, the god who smites from
      far."

Forthwith from all the host came loud acclaim:
"Take the rich ransom, reverence the priest."
The soul of Agamemnon, Atreus' son,
Alone it liked not: scornfully he bade him 30
Begone, and laid on him a hard command.

"Let me not find thee by the hollow ships
Or lingering now, old man, or yet again
Returning! Little shall avail thee then
Apollo's staff and emblem. For the girl, 35
I yield her not, till old age come on her
Ev'n in my home, in Argos, far away
From her own country; while she plies the loom

And tends my bed.   But go, provoke me not:
So peradventure shall we part in peace."   40

   So spake he; and the old man feared, and did
His bidding.   Mute he moved along the shore,
Among the noises of the boisterous sea:
And there, apart from men, prayed many a prayer
To gold-haired Leto's son, his King, Apollo.   45

   "Oh hear me, thou who standest round about
Chryse and sacred Cilla—mighty lord
Of Tenedos, who wield'st the silver bow!
Sminthian!   If ever I have builded up
From floor to roof a temple in thy praise,   50
Or ever burned to thee fat flesh of goats
And oxen: then accomplish this my prayer:
And let thy shafts avenge my tears upon the
      Greeks."

   So prayed he, and Apollo heard his prayer.
Yea from Olympus' heights he gat him down,   55
Wrath in his soul: upon his shoulder hung
The bow, and quiver covered all around.
Rang on the shoulder of the angry god
The arrows, as he stirred him: on he came
Like night: and by the ships he sate him down. 60
Twanged with a terrible twang the silver bow

As he sent forth one shaft.   And first of all
He visited the mules and swift-paced dogs:
Next at their own flesh levelling his keen dart
Smote, and for aye burned on the thick-strown
   pyres of slain.   65

 Nine days his arrows went abroad among
The host: and on the tenth Achilles called
The folk to council.   Moved thereto was he
By Herè, white-armed goddess; for she saw
Achaians dying, and it pitied her.   70
To whom when met, and ranged in meet conclave,
Achilles swift of foot arose and spake.

 " Oh sons of Atreus!   Now, I trow, will we
Turn us again, and drift—if flee we may
From death—ev'n thither whence we came: since
   war   75
And pestilence at once lay low the Greeks.
But hearken.   Seek we now some seer, or priest;
Or dream-interpreter;—dreams come from Zeus;—
To tell us what hath stirred Apollo thus.
If of a prayer, a sacrifice withheld,   80
He doth rebuke us: should it be his will,
Incense of lambs and goodliest of the goats
Accepting, to remove from us this plague."

He spake and sate him down. Then rose to them
High chief of augurs, Calchas, Thestor's son,   85
Who knew what is and was and is to be,
Who into Ilion piloted the Greeks,
By virtue of his art, Apollo's gift.
He friendly-minded rose and spake in the midst.

"Lo! thou command'st me, oh beloved of Zeus,
Achilles, to declare Apollo's wrath,   91
The far-off-smiting King. Now therefore I
Will speak: heed thou, and swear that of a truth
Freely thou'lt aid me both with tongue and arm.
Yea, for I think to anger one who rules   95
With might the Argives; and upon him wait
The Achaians. Now a vantage hath a King,
Let but a meaner man have angered him:
For though to-day his fury simmer down,
Yet thenceforth wrath abideth—till it work   100
Its purpose—in the bosom of the King.
Wherefore bethink thee, wilt thou succour me?"

And then Achilles swift of foot replied.
"The thing that thou dost know take heart and
    speak.
For by Apollo, loved of Zeus, whom thou,   105
Oh Calchas, worshipping interpretest
Unto the Danaans the things of God:—

The hand of no man out of all this host
Shall, while I live and see the light of day,
By yon broad ships be heavy upon thee: 110
Not if thou namest Agamemnon, him
Who vaunts himself this day the chiefest Greek."

    Then the good prophet took him heart and spake.
"Not of a prayer or of a sacrifice
Doth he rebuke: but for his servant's sake,   115
Whom Agamemnon did disdain, nor gave
His child, nor took her price: for this, I ween,
The Smiter deals us, and shall deal us, woe.
And heavy still shall be his wasting hand,
Till to her father dear the bright-eyed maid   120
Be giv'n, unbought, unransomed; and we bear
To Chryse holy sacrifice. This done,
It may be he will hear us and repent."

    He spake, and sate him down. Then rose to them
Broad-realmèd Agamemnon, Atreus' son,   125
A mighty man, sore angered. Fury filled
His heart's dark places: gleamed his eyes like fires.
First Calchas, boding mischief, he bespake.

    "Prophet of ill! Thou spak'st me never yet
A fair word. For thy soul loves evil still,   130

Nor aught good spak'st thou e'er, or brought'st to
    pass.
What prophesiest thou now before the host?
Sooth, that for this the Smiter works them woe;
Because I would not for rich ransom loose
The girl Chryseis. No! at home would I   135
Possess her: I prefer her to my wife,
My first-wed wife: she is Clytemnestra's match
In stature, shape, and mind, and handicraft.
Yet will I yield her up, if this be best.
I'd liefer see my people live than die.   140
Ye deck me straight a gift, lest I alone
Of Greeks ungifted be. That were not meet.
For see all men, my gift goes otherwhere."

  And then the swift Achilles answered him.
"Most honoured, most gain-greedy of mankind! 145
How may the generous Greeks find gifts for thee?
We wot not yet of public treasury:
The spoils of cities sacked we've parted all,
And should do ill re-levying these anew.
Now yield her to the god—and threefold we   150
And fourfold will repay thee, let but Zeus
Grant us to level yon fair walls of Troy."

  And royal Agamemnon made reply.

"Brave though thou art, great chief, yet play not
    thus
The knave: thou shalt not dupe me nor cajole. 155
Would'st thou—so thou have honour—that I sit
With empty hands? and bidd'st me yield her up?
Now if the generous Greeks will grant a gift—
One my soul loves, a meet equivalent—
Well: but if not, I'll take with mine own arm 160
Thine, or thine, Aias, or, Odysseus, thine,
And bear it off; and wrath mayhap he'll be
Whom I shall visit.—But of this anon.—
Launch we a dark ship on the great sea now,
Give her her tale of oars, and place on board 165
A hundred oxen, and embark therein
Fair-cheeked Briseis. And be one, a king,
Her captain; Aias, or Idomeneus,
Or great Odysseus, or, Achilles, thou
Most terrible of men; that thou mayest win 170
Back with thy rites the god who smites from far."

    Answered the swiftfoot chief with lowering brow:
"Oh clothed with shamelessness! oh selfish-souled!
What Greek will do ungrudging thy behests,
Speed on thy missions, bear the brunt of war? 175
I came not for the warrior Trojans' sake
Hither to fight. They owe no debt to me;
Ne'er in rich Phthia, nurse of mighty men,

Spoiled they my orchards:—for betwixt us lay
Long tracts of shadowy fell and sounding sea. 180
Shameless! 'Twas thou, thy pleasure, brought us
  here;
For Menelaüs, and thee, dog, to wreak
Vengeance on Troy—which things thou heedest
  not
Nor reck'st of. Lo! thou boast'st that thou wilt
  seize
With thine own arm my meed, my hardwon meed,
Assigned me by the children of the Greeks! 186
My gifts are not as thy gifts, when the Greeks
Lay low some goodly-peopled town of Troy:
My hands the burden of the weary war
Must bear; but *thy* share, when we part the spoil
Is greatest; I some small sweet morsel take 191
Back to my ships, when I am faint with strife.
But now I go to Phthia. Best to wend
Home with my beakèd ships. And scarce wilt
  thou—
Say I, disdainèd I—fill high thy cup 195
With treasure and with wealth, abiding here."

 Then answered Agamemnon, King of men.
"Go, if thy soul so prompts thee. I shall not
Say 'Stay' for my sake. I have others near
To prize me: first of all the all-wise Zeus. 200

Of Kings, the sons of heaven, I hate thee most.
Dear to thee aye are feuds and wars and strifes.
* Strong art thou? Then 'twas heaven that gave
   thy strength.
Go with thy ships and with thy followers home,
Rule Myrmidons.   I care not aught for thee 205
Nor for thy wrath.   And I will tell thee this.
Chryseis Phœbus takes from me: and her
I'll send, with *my* ships, and *my* followers, back.
But to thy tent I'll go, ev'n I, and take
Thy prize, the fair Briseis: that thou learn 210
How I am thy better: and that others shrink
To deem themselves my mates and cope with me."

 He spake.   And moved was Peleus' son: his
   heart
'Neath his rough breast was this way rent and that.
Should he, his keen sword drawing from his thigh,
Scatter the multitude and slay the King? 216
Or curb his spirit, and forego his wrath?
This was he turning in his brain and breast,
His great sword half unscabbarded; when lo!
From heaven Athenè came: a messenger 220
From white-armed Herè, to whose soul both chiefs
Were dear and precious.   In the rear she stood,
And grasped Achilles by his yellow hair:
Seen by him only—all the rest were blind.

He marvelling, turned round: and straightway knew
Pallas Athenè; dreadful gleamed her eyes.   226
And thus he spake to her with winged words.

"Why com'st thou, child of Ægis-armèd Zeus?
To witness Agamemnon's insolence?
This say I, and methinks 'twill come to pass.   230
One day he'll perish in his pride of heart."

   To whom the blue-eyed goddess spake again.
"To stay thine anger, if so be thou'lt hear
My voice, I came from heaven: a messenger
From white-armed Herè, to whose soul both chiefs
Are dear and precious. But leave off from strife,
And draw not forth the sword: but with thy tongue   237
Only revile him, as it needs must be.
For this *I* say, and this *shall* come to pass.
Trebled shall one day be thy rich reward   240
All through this insult. Hear then, and be calm."

   Again Achilles swift of foot replied.
"I must abide, oh goddess, by thy word,
Though angered sore in soul: for this is right.
To him that heeds them will the gods give ear."

   He said, and hearkening to Athenè, stayed   246
Ev'n on the silver hilt, his ponderous hand.

Heavenward meanwhile she had flown, to join her peers
Up in the home of Ægis-armèd Zeus.

   Then straight Achilles spake with harmful words
To Atreus' son, nor put his anger by.   251
"Oh gorged with wine! dog-faced, but hind at heart!
To arm thee with the people for the fray
Or with our captains crouch in ambuscade
Ne'er hadst thou courage. That were death to thee!   255
Better no doubt to range the broad host through,
And confiscate his prize who saith thee nay.
Thou glutton King! Thou rulest men of straw!
Else, son of Atreus, thou hadst bragged thy last.
But this I say and swear it with an oath.   260
Yea by this staff—where never leaf nor branch
May grow, since first 'twas sundered from the trunk
Upon the mountains, ne'er to blossom more—
(For that the axe hath stripped off bud and bark)—
Now in their hands the children of the Greeks   265
Bear it, who sit in judgment; whom Zeus calls
To guard the right; and men shall swear thereby—
The children of the Greeks shall one day long

All, for Achilles.   Thou shalt grieve, but find
No succour; while 'neath slaughtering Hector's,
      hand   270
Fall, and die, troops: but sit and gnash thy teeth,
Mad that thou sett'st at naught the noblest Greek."

   Achilles spake: and flung to earth his staff
Studded with golden nails; and sate him down.
The King sat o'er against him gathering wrath. 275
Then up sprang Nestor of the gracious tongue,
Clear orator of Pylos, from whose lips
Dropped music sweeter than the honeycomb.
Two generations now of speaking men
Had he seen born and bred and passed away   280
In sacred Pylos: and he ruled a third.
Who friendly-minded rose and spake in the midst.

   " Lo! a great sorrow comes upon our land.
Sure now would Priam and Priam's sons rejoice,
And every Trojan laugh within his heart,   285
Could he but learn how ye twain are at strife,
The first of Greeks in council and in war.
But hear me.   I can count more years than you.
Time was, when with a nobler race than ours
I mated: and they thought not scorn of me.   290
For ne'er yet saw I, nor shall see, their likes,
Cæneus, Pirithöus, Exadius,

Dryas, who led the people as a flock,
And Polyphemus, equal of the gods,
And Theseus, Ægeus' son, a very god.   295
These were the mightiest of the sons of earth.
Mightiest themselves, they fought with mightiest
    foes,
The Beasts of the Hill, and slew them horribly.
And I, to mate with these, from Pylos came,
From a far country; for they bade me come.   300
I fought for my own hand. No mortal man,
As men are now, would list to fight with such.
And they my counsels heard, my voice obeyed.
Ye too obey me. To obey is good.
Nor thou, thou mighty, take the maid away,   305
But quit her, since the Greeks first made her his.
Nor thou, Achilles, stand against the King
And strive: for never honour like to his
Had sceptred King, whose glory is of Zeus.
So, son of Atreus, stay thy rage. And him,   310
Our mighty rampart against evil war,
I do beseech to put his anger by."

  Then royal Agamemnon answered him.
"Naught hast thou said, oh sire, but what is meet.
But yonder man would overtop us all,   315
Be all men's lord and master, deal to all
Dictates, which one, at least, will scarce obey.

The gods who live for ever made him brave:
But did they thereby licence him to rail?"

   Then words of warning great Achilles spake. 320
"Call me a coward and a thing of naught,
If I yield all at every word of thine.
Talk thus to others—dictate not to me:
For I shall hearken to thy words no more.
But this I tell thee—cast it in thy mind!   325
I will not draw the sword for yon girl's sake
On thee or on another; since ye take
The thing ye gave. But of all else that's mine,
Treasured in my dark war-ship, not a thing
Without my licence shalt thou take or touch. 330
Doubt'st thou? Then try, that all this host may
    see.
Thy blood that instant spouts around my spear."

   So stood they face to face in wordy war.
And ended was the council at the ships.

   Achilles to his tents and stately fleet   335
Went with Patroclus, and his followers all.
The other launched a war-ship on the main,
Manned her with twenty oars, and stowed therein
A holy hecatomb, and seated there

Fair-cheeked Chryseis: and for captain, stept   340
On board Odysseus, he of many wiles.

  So they set forth and sailed the watery ways.
Then the King bade the people cleanse themselves.
They cleansed themselves, and cast into the sea
All their uncleanness: to Apollo next   345
They slew full hecatombs of bulls and goats
All by the barren waters: up to heaven
Went the sweet savour with the curling smoke.

  In such wise toiled the host.   Nor aught meanwhile
Paused Agamemnon in his threatened wrath.   350
But to Talthybius and Eurybates,
His heralds twain and busy servants, spake.

  "Go to Achilles' tent. Take thence and bring
The fair Briseis. If he say you nay,
I'll go, ev'n I, with yet a larger force,   355
And take her. And 'twill be the worse for him."

  So forth he sent them, charged with hard commands.
On, by the waters of the barren main
Unwillingly they fared: and reached at last
The vessels of the tented Myrmidons.   360

By his dark ship they found him in his tent;—
Little Achilles joyed at seeing them;—
Awe-struck and trembling they before the chief
Stood; nor accosted him, nor uttered sound:
But he knew well their purpose, and began.   365

" Hail, heralds, messengers of Zeus and men !
Draw near. I blame not you; I blame the King,
Who sent you here for fair Briseis' sake.
But come, oh prince Patroclus, lead her forth,
And give her to their hand. And be these twain
My witnesses before the blessed gods   371
And mortal men and that untoward King :—
When one day there ariseth need of me
Their shield from foul destruction! For the King
Raves, a doomed madman; nor can look at once
Before him and behind, and see whose arm   376
Let the Greeks battle by the ships and live."

He said. Patroclus his loved lord obeyed,
And led the fair Briseis from the tent,
And gave her to their hand. And straightway they
Made for the Achaian ships; and with them fared   381
The damsel all unwilling. But the chief
Wept; and from all his fellows gat apart,
And by the gray seas sate him down, and gazed

c

Far o'er the purpling waters: and to her 385
Who bore him lifted up his hands and prayed.

"Mother! Thou brought'st me forth not long
  to live:
Therefore should Zeus, the Thunderer, of high
  heaven,
Put glory in my hand. But not a whit
Honours he me: yea scorned am I of one, 390
Broad-realmèd Agamemnon, Atreus' son;
With his own arm he seized, and hath, my gift."

Weeping he spake. His queenly mother heard,
'Neath ocean sitting by her ancient sire:
And rose from the gray waters as a mist, 395
And sate her down beside her weeping son,
Fondled his hand, and spake, and called him by his
  name.

"Why weep'st thou, Son? What grief is on
  thy soul?
Speak, and naught hide: that *I* too know this
  thing."

And with a heavy groan the swift chief spake.
"Shall I tell all to thee who know'st it all? 401
We came to sacred Thebes, Eetion's Thebes,

And spoiled her, and brought hither all the spoil.
And fairly did the children of the Greeks,
Part it amongst them, and for Atreus' son 405
Chose out fair-cheeked Chryseis. Thereupon
Came Chryses, priest of him who smites from far,
Ev'n to the war-ships of the steel-clad Greeks,
With ransom measureless to buy his child:
And in his hands Apollo's emblem sat, 410
The Smiter's, high upon a staff of gold.
To all the Greeks he prayed, but chief of all
To Atreus' sons, twin captains of the host.—
Forthwith from all the Greeks came loud acclaim:
' Take the rich ransom, reverence the priest.' 415
The soul of Agamemnon, Atreus' son,
Alone it liked not: scornfully he bade him
Begone, and laid on him a hard command.

   " Back went in wrath that old man: and his
      prayer
Apollo heard, because he loved him well: 420
And hurled his fell shaft on us; heaps on heaps
The people died. Amongst Achaia's hosts
His arrows went abroad. Then spake the seer,
Who knew it well, the Far-destroyer's will. 424

   " My voice first bade them reconcile the god.
But rage seized Atreus' son. He rose up straight,
And threatened that which, lo! is brought to pass.
For her the keen-eyed Greeks are carrying now

To Chryse in yon war-ship: but that other,
Briseis—whom the children of the Greeks 430
Gave to my hand—the heralds from my tent
Have but this instant taken, and are gone.—
Now stand by thy brave son, if stand thou mayest.
Hie thee to heaven; pray Zeus—if ever word
Or deed of thine made glad the soul of Zeus:—
For in my father's halls I have heard thee tell 436
Of times when of immortals thou alone
Didst shield from foul destruction him who dwells
In darkness and in clouds, Cronion named;
When Herè, Pallas, and Poseidon—all 440
The blessed gods—would bind him. Thou didst come,
Goddess, and loose his bonds, and summon quick
Into the broad heaven him of hundred hands—
Gods call him Briareus, Ægeon men—
Him who excels in bodily force his sire. 445
By Zeus he sate down, glorying in his might.
Cowed were the blessed gods, and bound him not.
 "Remember this: sit near him: clasp his knees:
Pray that he find some way to succour Troy:
And them—the Greeks—push ev'n to their ships' sterns, 450
To die amid the waters, that all know
How much they owe their King; and Atreus' son,

Broad-realmèd Agamemnon, learn how mad
Was he, to set at naught the noblest Greek."

And Thetis answered, letting fall a tear.　　455
"Why did I rear thee, born—alas my son!—
In sorrow? Would that tearless and unpained
Thou wert sitting by thy ships: for lo! thy life
Is but a little while, a little while.
Now passing sad thy days, as passing brief:　　460
Surely in evil hour I brought thee forth.
But with this tale I go to those snowpeaks,
To Zeus, whose plaything is the thunderbolt,
Will he but hear me. Thou by thy swift ships
Sit, curse the Greeks, and stay thy hand from war.
For Zeus to the good Æthiops yesterday,　　466
To ocean, went, with all the gods, to feast.
The twelfth day he'll return Olympusward.
Then to his brassfloored palace will I go,
And clasp his knees; and surely he'll repent."　　470

She said: and vanishing left him, vexed at heart
All for that graceful maiden, whom by force
And violence they had ta'en.

　　　　　　　　　　　　Odysseus reached

Chryse meanwhile, with holy sacrifice.
Now, the deep harbour gained, they furled and
    stowed   475
In the dark ship their sails; placed mast in crutch,
Lowered on stays all swiftly; and the rowers
Into her moorings rowed her.   Anchor-stones
They cast out next, and made the hawsers fast,
And leapt out on the sea-strand; and bore forth 480
The holy sacrifice: and last stepped out
From the sea-travelling ship that damsel fair.
Whom to the altar led the wily chief,
Placed in her father's hand her hand, and spake.

"Priest! Atreus' son hath sent me, King of
    men,   485
To bring thy child, and holy sacrifice
Make for the Greeks; and reconcile the King,
Who now brings many sorrows on the host."

    He spake, and gave her to his hand: who took
His child rejoicing.   Swiftly then they ranged 490
Round the fair altar that brave sacrifice:
Held up, with washen hands, the barley grains:
And then with lifted arm the priest made solemn
    prayer.

"Oh! hear me, thou who standest round about

Chryse and sacred Cilla: mighty lord 495
Of Tenedos, who wield'st the silver bow!
Surely thou heard'st me heretofore; and sore,
To honour me, didst plague Achaia's hosts.
And now accomplish this, ev'n this my prayer.
From foul destruction shield this day the Greeks."

So spake he: and Apollo heard his prayer. 501
They having knelt, and strewed the barley grains,
Drew back the victim's head, and slew, and flayed,
And cut the thighs off, and around them wrapped
The fat in layers, and sprinkled flesh thereon. 505
These the sire burned on wood; poured sparkling
    wine,
The warriors standing by with fivepronged forks:
They burned the thighs, and tasted of the heart,
And mashed and fixed on spits the residue,
And made roast cunningly, and drew all off. 510
At last the feast was decked. They ceased from toil,
And supped, nor aught lacked at that equal board.
And when the lust of meat and drink was gone,
The warriors filled the goblets to the brim,
And, first oblation made, they served to all. 515
With songs the livelong day they soothed the god,
Those Grecian warriors. Sweet the hymns they
    sang.
The Far-destroyer listened and was glad.

But when the sun set and the dusk came on,
They slept beside the cables of the ship. 520
And when Morn's daughter, rosy-fingered Dawn,
Rose, for the broad Achaian host they steered:
The Far-destroyer sent a steady gale.
They raised the mast, and spread white sails thereon.
Bellied the sails; and purpling round the keel 525
Sounded the dark waves as the ship went on:
She scudded o'er the seas and made her way.
They, when they had reached the broad Achaian host,
Drew the dark ship to land; high on the sands
They left her, and set great stones underneath, 530
And went home each man to his tent and ship.

Meanwhile the swift-foot chief, great Peleus' son,
By his sea-travelling ships sat nursing wrath:
To the high council went not day by day,
Went not to war: but wasted his sweet soul, 535
Abiding there, and dreamed of turmoil and of strife.

The twelfth day dawned: and to Olympus trooped,
Zeus in the van, the ever-living gods.
Thetis forgat not then her son's behests;
But mounted on the sea-wave, and in mist 540
Rose to the great heaven and the holy mount.
Seated apart she found the All-seeing One,

On many-peaked Olympus' topmost crag:
Sat at his feet, with one hand clasped his knees,
With the other held his beard; and prayed and
  spake   545
Thus to the son of Cronos, royal Zeus.

"Zeus! Sire! If ever word or deed of mine
Among the immortals welcome was to thee,
Accomplish this my prayer. Exalt my son,
Whose days are briefer than are other mens'. 550
Of Agamemnon now is he disdained;
He took, he hath, his gift. But thou, who dwell'st
In the high heaven, exalt him, all-wise Zeus!
Put victory on the Trojans, till the Greeks
Exalt my son, and spread abroad his praise." 555

 She spake. Cloud-circled Zeus said ne'er a word.
Long he sat voiceless. Thetis to his knees
Clung as the flesh clings, and she spake again.

 "Now bow thy head, and pledge thy changeless
  word,
Or else refuse—for fears come not nigh thee. 560
Say that of all the gods thou hold'st me least."

 Spake, big with anger, then cloud-circled Zeus.
"Lo! there is woe to be if I must strive

With Herè, whensoe'er she taunts and rails.
Ev'n now she wars with me from day to day   565
Before the gods, and saith I fight for Troy.
Now go thou hence again, lest Herè know
This thing; and leave the issue in my hand.
Yea, that thou mayest have faith, I bow my head.
For this is my great token with the gods.   570
Irrevocable, true, each word of mine,
Sure of its purpose, when I bow my head."

   Cronion spake: his dark brows bent, and bowed.
From his immortal head fell rippling down
The glory of his hair.   The great rock reeled.   575

   Such counsel took those twain, and parted.   She
Plunged from the bright heaven into ocean's depths,
And Zeus went homeward.   Rose up all the gods
And stood before the Sire.   None dared abide
His coming; all stood up and fronted him.   580
High on his throne he sate him.   Herè marked:
And well she knew what counsel he had ta'en
With that old sea-god's silvery-footed child.
Forthwith in bitterness she spake to Zeus.

   "And which of all the gods, oh wily one,   585

Was partner in thy counsels? Aye thou lov'st
To sit, and scheme, and settle, far from me.
And never yet didst thou of thy free-will
Deign to tell *me* one word of thy designs."

Then spake to her the sire of gods and men. 590
"Look not, oh Herè, all my mind to know.
Hard were such knowledge, though thou art my
    wife.
That which 'tis fit for thee to hear, nor god
Nor man shall learn before thee. But such plans
As I may plan, and hide from every god— 595
Ask not of these things straitly nor inquire."

Then answered Herè, the gazelle-eyed Queen.
"Dread son of Cronos, have I heard thee right?
Long time too little asked I or inquired;
Thou plotting that which pleased thee, undisturbed.
But now sore fears my soul, lest thou be duped 601
By that old sea-god's silvery-footed child.
Mist-clad she sat by thee and clasped thy knees:
And thou, as I suspect, didst bow thy head,
In token that thou would'st exalt her son, 605
And by the Achaian ships make many fall."

Then spake in answer cloud-encircled Zeus.

"Wayward! thou wilt aye 'suspect.' I know thee
    well.
But all thou wilt not compass—farther still
Wilt set me from thee.   All the worse for thee.
Sit down, be silent, and obey my words: 611
Lest all the gods heaven holds avail thee naught,
Let me but lift my matchless arm on thee."

  He spake; and trembled the gazelle-eyed Queen;
Silent sat down, and bent her to his will.   615
Then with big wrath were swelled the heavenly ones
In Zeus's palace: till Hephæstus rose,
The great Artificer, and welcome words
To white-armed Herè spake, his mother dear.

  "Woe shall there be, intolerable woe,   620
If ye twain battle thus for mortals' sake,
And stir up war in heaven.   All joyless then
Shall seem the fair feast, since the worst prevails.
But I my mother warn (though wise is she)
To pleasure Zeus our sire: lest he should strive
A second time with her, and mar our feast.   626
What if the lord of lightning from her seat
Should choose to hurl her? for none else is strong.
But thou with softest words approach him now.
Straightway the heavenly one will smile on us."

  He said, and leapt up, and a ponderous cup 631
Placed in his mother's hand, and spake to her.

"Be patient, mother, and though vexed, endure:
Lest mine eyes see her smitten whom I love.
Then shall I sorrow, yet may aid thee naught: 635
Hard 'tis to fight against the heavenly one.
Yea, for aforetime did he hurl me down,
Burning to aid thee, from the gates of heaven,
Grasped by one foot. All day I fell and fell,
And lighted at the setting of the sun   640
In Lemnos. Little life was in me then.
There lighting I became the Sintians' care."

   He spake. The white-armed goddess smiled and
      took
The cup her son gave in her hand: while he
Filled for the others all, from left to right,   645
And poured the luscious nectar from the bowl.
Quenchless the laughter of the blessed gods,
To see him puff and pant about the hall.

   So they the live-long day, till set of sun,
Feasted, nor lacked aught at that equal board: 650
Lacked not Apollo's lovely lyre, lacked not
The Muses, whose sweet voice took up the song.

   But when the bright sun's glory had gone down,
Ready for rest they parted each to his home:
To where the Crippled Deity for each   655

Had wrought a palace with a cunning hand.
The Lord of lightning went and laid him down
Where he had slept full oft at sweet Sleep's call:
Thither ascended he, and there he slept;
And golden-thronèd Herè by his side.   660

BOOK II.

SO all else—gods, and charioted chiefs—
   Slept the night through. But sweet sleep bound not Zeus;
Pondering what way Achilles to exalt,
And by the Achaian ships make many fall.

   This to his soul the fairest counsel seemed;   5
To send to Atreus' son an evil Dream:
And to the Dream he spake with wingèd words.

   "Go, evil Dream, to yon Greek war-ships; seek
The tent of Agamemnon, Atreus' son;
And tell him, truly, all I tell to thee.   10

Say, 'Arm right speedily thy unshorn Greeks;
This hour is Ilion and her broad streets thine.
For lo! no longer are the immortals—they
Whose home is heaven—divided. Herè's prayer 14
Hath bent them all; and woes are nigh to Troy.'"

He spake. The Dream, obedient, went his way;
Came swiftly to the war-ships of the Greeks,
And sought out Atreus' son :—(at rest he lay,
Divine sleep floating o'er him, in his tent:)—
And stood above his head; in form most like 20
To Nestor, Neleus' son : of all who sat
In council Agamemnon ranked him first.
In such shape spake to him the heaven-sent Dream.

"Sleep'st thou, O son of Atreus? son of one
At heart a warrior, tamer of the steed? 25
Not all night long a counsellor should sleep,
A people's guard, whose cares are manifold.
Now hear me. Zeus's messenger am I;
Who, though far off, yet cares, yet grieves for thee.
He bids thee arm in haste the unshorn Greeks; 30
Saying, 'Now is Ilion and her broad streets thine.
For lo! no longer are the immortals—they
Whose home is heaven—divided. Herè's prayer
Hath bent them all; and woes are nigh to Troy,'
Woes which Zeus sends. This ponder in thy mind:

Nor be the captive of forgetfulness, 36
So soon as thou shalt wake from honeyed sleep."

   He spake: and parting left him there, to muse
In secret on the thing that might not be.
For in that day he thought to scale Priam's walls,
And knew not, simple one, the wiles of Zeus; 41
How he would bring more woes, more groanings yet,
On Trojan and on Greek in hard-fought fields.
He woke: and sate erect—the heavenly voice
Still floating o'er him: donned his tunic soft 45
And fair and new: flung o'er him his great robe,
Harnessed fair sandals to his shining feet,
And o'er his shoulder swung his silver-studded sword.
And took his fathers' sceptre in his hand,
Imperishable aye: and sought therewith 50
The vessels of the brazen-coated Greeks.

   At broad Olympus' gate stood sacred Dawn,
To Zeus and all the gods proclaiming light.
Then the king bade his shrill-tongued heralds go
And summon council-ward the unshorn Greeks; 55
Who came all swiftly at their heralding.

   But first a council of high elders sat

At Nestor's ship, the Pylos-nurtured king.
Thither he called them: there framed shrewd advice.

"Hear, friends! In holy night a heaven-sent
    Dream   60
Came near me while I slept: in face, and form,
And bulk, it seemed great Nestor's counterpart.
Above my head it stood, and spake to me.
'Sleep'st thou, O son of Atreus? son of one
At heart a warrior, tamer of the steed?   65
Not all night long a counsellor should sleep,
A people's guard, whose cares are manifold.
Now hear me. Zeus's messenger am I;
Who, though far off, yet cares, yet grieves for thee.
He bids thee arm in haste thy unshorn Greeks;   70
Saying, Now is Ilion and her broad streets thine.
For lo! no longer are the immortals—they
Whose home is heaven—divided. Herè's prayer
Hath bent them all; and woes are nigh to Troy,
Woes which Zeus sends. This ponder in thy mind.'
So spake the Dream; and spread his wings, and
    fled.   76
And sweet sleep gat from me. But up and look
How we may arm for war Achaia's sons.
And first I will prove them, as is meet, with words,
And bid them deck for flight their oarèd ships. 80
Ye, wending separate ways, forbid their flight."

He spake, and sat him down. Then Nestor rose,
That Nestor who in sandy Pylos reigned.
Who friendly-minded rose and spake in the midst.

"Friends! lords and captains of the Argive
   hosts! 85
Now had another Greek this vision told,
We had said, 'Thou liest;' and put us far from
  him.
But lo! he saw it, of Achaians all
Who vaunts him noblest. Nay then, up and look
How we may arm for war Achaia's sons." 90

He spake; and slowly from the council moved.
They rose, and followed in their leaders' wake,
Those sceptred kings; the host flocked after them.
As when, from some rock's hollow, swarm on swarm,
Rise multitudes of thickly-thronging bees: 95
And hang in clusters o'er the flowers of spring,
And fly in myriads, this way some, some that;
They in such multitudes from tent and ship,
Skirting the bottomless sea-sand, marched in troops
To council. With them sped a voice of fire 100
Bidding them on: Zeus sent it: and they met.
Unquietly they met: earth groaned beneath
The trampling of the hosts as they sate down:
And there was tumult. Then did heralds nine

Shout out, entreating them to stay their strife, 105
And listen to the kings, the sons of heaven.
In haste they sate down, halting each in his place,
And stilled their noise. Then Agamemnon rose,
Bearing that sceptre which Hephæstus wrought,
And gave unto Croníon, royal Zeus. 110
Zeus to the courier-god, the Argus-slayer:
Hermes to Pelops, lasher of the steed:
Pelops to Atreus, shepherd of the host:
And Atreus to Thyestes rich in lambs
Dying bequeathed it. And Thyestes last 115
Gave it to Agamemnon's arm to wield,
And be the lord of Argos and the isles.
Leaning whereon he spake before the host.

"Friends, sons of Ares, mighty men of Greece!
Me hath Zeus bound to heaviness and woe. 120
Once (reckless one!) he swore, and bowed his head,
That I should raze Troy's walls and get me home.
But mischief doth he plot against me now:
Sends me to Argos, shamed; for I have slain
Much people. Thus then fare the favourites 125
Of Zeus the all-mighty: who hath bent the crests
Of many cities; yea, and who shall bend
The crests of many more; for strong is he.
Our sons shall one day hear it, and cry ' Shame!
Did Greece's chosen in such numbers come, 130

To battle, and to fight a bootless fight'—
(For still we see no end)—'against a few?'
Few, say I. For suppose we struck a truce,
Trojans and Greeks, and numbered each our hosts:
They singling all who sit beside their hearths, 135
We parting into companies of ten;
And to each ten one Trojan served the wine:—
Unserved would sit full many a company.
So do the Greeks exceed in multitude
The Trojans in yon city. Yet have they 140
Allies from many cities; sworded chiefs,
Who thwart me mightily, and say me nay,
When I would level those fair walls of Troy.
Nine of the years of royal Zeus are past:
And lo! the rigging of our ships is torn, 145
Rotted their timbers; and our wives, I ween,
And lisping children sit within our halls,
And wait us: and our work, for which we came
To Troy, is unaccomplished. Nay but up
And do my bidding. Set we sail and fly 150
To our dear fatherland: for never more
May we deem Ilion and her broad streets ours."

He spake; and stirred the inmost soul of all
The broad host: all save those who knew his wiles.
Then surged the council. On the Icarian main 155
So surge great sea-waves, when the clouds of Zeus

Let loose upon them winds from North and East.
And as the West wind meets the standing corn,
And stirs it to its depths, and ravens on,
A hurricane; and all the ears bow down:— 160
Ev'n so was stirred the council. Seaward they
Rushed with a cry. The dust rose under-foot,
In volumes. Each called each, to lend a hand
And drag the vessels down to the great sea.
Cleared were the trenches: rose to heaven their
    cry, 165
As, homeward-bound, they dragged their ships
    from shore.

Then had the Greeks fled home before their
    time;
But Herè to Athenè spake and said:
"Oh me! oh child of Ægis-armèd Zeus,
Untiring one! shall Argives thus flee home, 170
Riding the broad seas, to their fatherland;
And leave, that Priam and his hosts may boast,
Helen of Argos—for whom here in Troy,
Far from his fatherland, died many a Greek? 174
Now range the armies of the brass-clad Greeks:
And with thy soft words stay them, man by man;
Nor seaward let them drag their rocking ships."

She spake; the blue-eyed maid gave ear to her:

Yea, from Olympus' heights went hurrying down,
And came to the Greek war-ships speedily.   180
And there she found Odysseus, Zeus's match
In cunning, standing still.   He had not laid
A finger on his dark and oarèd ship;
For sorrow sat upon his heart and soul.
Standing beside him spake the blue-eyed maid. 185

"Laertes' son ! the man of many wiles !
What ! leaping thus into your oarèd ships
Shall ye flee home unto your fatherland :
And leave, that Priam and his hosts may boast,
Helen of Argos—for whom here in Troy,   190
Far from his fatherland, died many a Greek ?
Now range the armies of the brass-clad Greeks ;
And with thy soft words stay them, man by man,
Nor seaward let them drag their rocking ships."

She spake.   He knew her voice who spake to
     him :   195
Girt him for speed, and flung his robe away.
Eurybates the herald picked it up,
That Ithacan, his servant.   He himself
Came straight to Agamemnon Atreus' son ;
And took from him the sceptre of his sires,   200
Imperishable aye ; and sought therewith
The vessels of the brazen-coated Greeks.

Oft as he met a king, or foremost man,
He checked him, halting near, with softest words.

"Fair sir! thou shouldst not cower as doth a
    knave;   205
Now seat thyself, and likewise seat thy hosts.
Thou know'st not yet the mind of Atreus' son.
Now proves he, but anon shall plague, the Greeks.
We know not, all, the purport of his words
In council. Should his wrath wax hot, and work
A mischief to the children of the Greeks!   211
For high the soul of kings, the sons of heaven.
Of Zeus their glory: wise Zeus loves them well."

Then when he saw, or heard uplift his voice,
One of the people: with his sceptre he   215
Would thrust at him, and shout that he might hear.

"Sirrah! sit down, and stir not, but obey
Thy betters. Helpless and unwarlike thou,
Of none account in council or in strife.
We may not, look you, all be monarchs here.   220
The multitude of rulers bodes but ill.
Be one our lord, our king; to whom the son
Of wily Cronos gave it: sceptre gave
And sovereignty, that he should reign o'er us."

Ev'n thus he dealt his mandates through the host;

And councilward they rushed from tent and ship.
The noise was as the noise of boisterous seas, 227
That break on some broad beach, and ocean howls.

So all sate down, and halted each in his place.
Still one—Thersites of ungoverned tongue— 230
Brawled on. Much store had he of scurrilous words,
Idle and scurrilous words, to hurl at kings:
Aught that he deemed the Greeks would hear and
    laugh.
To Troy's gates none had come so base as he.
Bow-legged he was, and halted on one foot: 235
His shoulders, hunched, encroached upon his chest;
And bore a peaked head—scant hairs grew thereon.
Achilles and Odysseus most he loathed ;
At them railed aye: but Agamemnon now
He taunted in shrill treble. All the Greeks 240
Were angered sore, and vexed within their soul.
At Agamemnon did he rail and cry.

"What lack'st thou ? Why complainest, Atreus'
    son ?
With brass thy tents abound: and in them wait
Many and peerless maidens ; whom we Greeks, 245
Whene'er we take a town, choose first for thee.
Ask'st thou yet gold ; which one mayhap shall
    bring—

A tamer of the steed—from Ilion,
To buy his son? whom peradventure I,
Or some Greek else hath bound and made his
    prize?   250
Or yet a damsel to ascend thy bed,
Kept for thine own self? Nay, unkingly 'tis
To bring this mischief on Achaia's sons.
Oh cowards! oh base and mean—not men, but
    maids!   254
Home fare we with our ships: and leave him here,
To gorge him with his honours—here in Troy:
And see if we will fight for him or no.
For him, who scorned one better far than he;
For his hand took, he hath, Achilles' gift.
Yet naught Achilles frets, good easy man.   260
Else, son of Atreus, thou hadst bragged thy last."

So chode Thersites him who led the host.
But straightway was Odysseus at his side,
And, scowling, with hard words encountered him.

"Thou word-entangler! Clear thy voice and
    shrill: 265
Yet think not singly to contend with kings.
I say no mortal, out of all that came
With Atreus' sons to Troy, is base as thou.
Wherefore thou should'st not lift thy voice and roar

And rail at kings, thy watchword still 'Return.'
We know not yet the end: whether for weal 271
Or woe we shall return, we sons of Greece.
So thou at Agamemnon, Atreus' son,
The shepherd of the host, must sit and rail,
For that on him the mighty men of Greece 275
Heap gifts: and cut him to the heart with words.
But this I say, and this shall come to pass.
Forget thyself, as now thou hast, again:—
And—from Odysseus' shoulders drop his head,
Nor be he called Telemachus's sire, 280
If this hand strip not all thy garments off,
Mantle and tunic, and lay bare thy loins,
And send thee to the war-ships, wailing loud;
Driven from the council with the blows of shame."

He spake: and with his sceptre smote his back
And shoulders. Writhed Thersites, and the tears
Came gushing: and a crimson wale appeared, 287
Where lit the golden sceptre, on his back.
Down sate he, trembling all and woe-begone;
And dried his eyes; and looked round helplessly.
Then laughed they fairly, tho' their souls were
    grieved, 291
And each unto his neighbour looked and said;

"Now many a brave deed hath Odysseus done;

Fathered fair counsels, reared the crest of war:
But bravest this which he hath wrought to-day, 295
Hushing that scorner's speech, who smites with words.
Sure never more that o'er-great soul of his
Shall raise him up to gibe and scoff at kings."

   So spake the people. Then Odysseus rose,
Sacker of towns, his sceptre in his hand.   300
The blue-eyed goddess in a herald's shape
Stood near: that all, both high and low, might hear
His counsel, and acquaint them with his mind.
He friendly-minded rose and spake in the midst.

   "Prince! Atreus' son! Lo! now they will that thou   305
Should'st do in all men's eyes a deed of shame:
Nor keep the pledge they pledged, when on their way
Hither from Argos, pasture of the steed,
That thou should'st raze yon walls and get thee home:
But ev'n as babes or widowed wives, they wail 310
Each to his fellow, 'Get we home again.'
And such indeed the toil we have toiled, that one
Might get him home in very weariness.

For let a man abide one single month,
He and his fair-oared ship—let blast and storm 315
And angry ocean keep him prisoner—
Far from his wife: and sad shall be his soul.
But we—we see the ninth year rolling on,
And bide here still. Wherefore small blame to them 319
That fret beside their ships. And yet 'twere base
To stay, and stay, and then go empty home.
Bear, friends: bide yet a little: till we learn
If Calchas speak true prophecies or false.
For this we know full well:—bear witness all
Not yet led captive by the Powers of death:— 325
When—'twas as yesterday,—to Aulis flocked
Achaia's ships, the messengers of woe
To Priam and to Troy; and round about
The fountain, at the holy altar, we
Made to the immortals choicest sacrifice, 330
By the fair plane, whence glistening waters rolled:
Then saw we a great sign. A snake whose back
Was blood-red; sent, of him who dwells in heaven,
From darkness into light—a fearful thing—
Sprang sudden from the altar to the plane. 335
Whereon were young birds sitting, tiny things,
On the tree-top: and cowered amidst the leaves;
Eight of them: she, who bare the brood, made nine.
He ate them; chirping, all eight, piteously;

And as the mother fluttered round and round 340
And wailed her offspring; darting from his coils
He seized the shrieking creature by the wing.
And when he had eaten bird and brood, the god
Appeared, and wrought in him a miracle.
As we stood marvelling to see such things, 345
Wise Cronos' son transformed him into stone.
Such portents mingling with our sacrifice,
Then forthwith Calchas prophesied and spake.
'What struck ye speechless, oh ye unshorn Greeks?
To us this mighty sign wise Zeus hath shewed, 350
Late coming, late in its accomplishment,
The fame whereof shall never pass away.
Ev'n as that serpent ate up bird and brood,
Eight of them; she who bare the brood made nine;—
Shall we, for years so many warring here, 355
Take Ilion and her broad streets in the ninth.'
So spake he, and behold! it comes to pass.
Nay then, abide, O bravely-harnessed Greeks,
Here, until yon great citadel be ours."

   He spake, and from the Greeks a mighty cry 360
Went up: and all the vessels round about
Rang fiercely at the shouting of the hosts,
Who liked divine Odysseus' counsel well.
To whom spake Nestor the Gerenian knight.

"Oh gods! Your speech is as the speech of babes
Too young to busy them with warfare yet.   366
Where then our oaths, our contracts? Fling we now
Our plots and manly counsels to the flames,
Our pledges pledged in wine, and our right hands
Wherein we trusted. For behold! we strive   370
Idly with words; and, long time tarrying here,
See yet no end. But thou, oh Atreus' son,
Stablished of purpose ev'n as heretofore,   373
Lead on the Argives still through hard-fought fields:
While they drop off, those two or three, who sit
Aloof, and plot—(and shall accomplish naught)—
To turn them Argos-ward, or e'er we see
If Ægis-armèd Zeus keep faith or no.
Yea for I say Cronion bowed his head,   379
The all-mighty, in that day when first the Greeks
Stept on their swift ships, messengers of blood
And death to Troy—and, thundering to the right,
Signalled fair fortune. So let none speed home,
Till each hath lain beside a Trojan wife,
And Helen's cares and anguish are avenged.   385
But whoso longs amazingly for home,
Let him upon his dark and oarèd ship
Lay hold; and ere his fellows, drop and die.
But do thou, King, consider and obey.
Not idle are the words which Nestor speaks. 390
Tell into clans and tribes, oh King, thy men:

That clan may stand by clan, and tribe by tribe.
So shalt thou—if the Greeks obey thy voice—
See which be base, which brave, of all the host,
Leaders and led:—for singly they will fight:—395
And know if it be Fate, or man's unskill
And cowardice, that bars thy road to Troy."

    And royal Agamemnon spake again.
"Yea, and in council none is like to thee
Old man, of all the children of the Greeks.   400
O Zeus, O Phœbus, and Athenè! would
I had ten such counsellors! Soon would bow yon
       walls,
By our arm ta'en and sacked. But Cronos' son
Makes woe my portion. Ægis-armèd Zeus
Doth cast my lot in bootless feuds and strifes. 405
Lo! for a girl's sake strive with warring tongues
I and Achilles—my wrath roused the strife.
Should but we twain be one in purpose, then
Not for an hour shall linger Ilion's doom.
But break ye now your fast, and then to war. 410
Let each whet well his spear, and hold his shield
Ready, feed well his swift-foot steeds, and look,
For battle bound, his chariot o'er and o'er:
That in stern war we strive the livelong day.
For rest there shall be none, no not an hour, 415
Until night coming part the strong men's arms.

The leathern fastenings of the broad-orbed shield
Shall drip with sweat; the hands that close around
The spear-shaft falter: steeds shall drip with sweat,
Drawing their polished cars. And should I mark
One, minded by his beaked ships to abide,   421
Aloof from battle—slender hope were his
Thenceforth, to 'scape the vulture and the dog."

  He spake. The Argives gave a mighty roar.
So roars a billow—by the South wind stirred,   425
On some high beach—against a jutting rock,
Lashed evermore by waves from every wind
Of heaven, on this side gathering and on that.
They rose, and sprang forth, parting each to his ship;
And, kindling each his tent-fire, brake their
      fast: 430
And to the gods who live for ever prayed,
This one or that, with sacrifice, to flee
Death and the moil of war. An ox meanwhile
Did Agamemnon slaughter, King of men,
Fat, in its fifth year, to most mighty Zeus: 435
And called the reverend chiefs of all the Greeks,
First Nestor, and the Prince Idomeneus;
Then the two Aiases, and Tydeus' son;
Odysseus sixth, in craft a match for Zeus.
Unbid the clear-voiced Menelaüs came;   440
His soul well wotted how his brother toiled.

Ranged round the ox, they raised the barley grains,
And royal Agamemnon spake in prayer.

" Most high, most mighty, dweller in the heaven,
Zeus, hid in clouds and darkness! ere yon sun 445
Set, and the dark draw on, may I have laid
Priam's blackening palace low, and Priam's gates
Burned with avenging flame: and rent the clothes
Of Hector with the sword's edge on his breast,
And round about him seen much people fall 450
In dust, and with their teeth lay hold on earth."

He spake. Cronion heard not yet his prayer:
His offering took, but multiplied his woe.
They having knelt, and strewed the barley grains,
Drew back the victim's head, and slew, and flayed, 455
And cut the thighs off, and around them wrapped
The fat in layers, and sprinkled flesh thereon.
And these they burned on leafless logs; and held,
Pierced with their knives, the entrails o'er the flame.
They burned the thighs, and tasted of the heart, 460
And mashed and fixed on spits the residue,
And made roast cunningly, and drew all off.
And when the lust of meat and drink was gone,
First spake out Nestor, the Gerenian knight.

"Most glorious Agamemnon, King of men! 465
Sit we not talking here, nor still forego
The thing that lo! heaven putteth in our hand.
But up. Let heralds of the brass-mailed Greeks
Cry, and collect the folk from ship and ship:
While through the broad host thus in multitude 470
We go, and swiftly bid keen war awake."

He spake. Nor heedless was the King of men.
Forthwith he bade his shrill-voiced heralds go
And summon council-ward the unshorn Greeks,
Who came all swiftly at their heralding. 475
Round Atreus' son the kings, the sons of heaven,
Ranged and arrayed them. And Athenè helped,
The blue-eyed maid, her Ægis in her hand,
That precious thing, that grows not old nor fades.
A hundred tassels hang from it, all gold, 480
All deftly wov'n; worth each a hecatomb.
Therewith she ran wild-eyed amid the host,
Bidding them on: and roused in every breast
The will to fight and cease not. And behold!
Sweeter to them seemed warfare, than to steer 485
Their hollow ships unto their fatherland.

As on the mountain peaks destroying flame
Fires a great forest; far is seen the glare:—

From off the glorious steel the full-orbed light 489
Went skyward on through ether as they marched.

And even as great hosts of wingèd birds,
Storks, cranes, or long-necked swans, flit here and there
In Asian meadow round Caÿster's stream
On jubilant wing: and, making van-ward each,
Scream, that the whole mead rings:—so poured their hosts 495
From tent and ship into Scamander's plain.
Earth underfoot rang fiercely, to the tramp
Of warriors and of horses. There they stood
Upon Scamander's richly-blossomed plain,
Innumerable, as flowers and leaves in spring. 500

And as great hosts of swarming flies that flit
In springtime, when the milk is in the cans,
About the herdsman's hut: so numerous stood
Before Troy's ranks the Greeks upon the plain,
And thirsted to destroy them utterly. 505

And as the goatherds sunder easily
Broad droves, as one flock feeding: even so
Their captains marshalled each his company
For war; amidst them Atreus' royal son,
In eye and front like Zeus, Ares in bulk, 510

In chest Poseidon. As among the herd
The bull ranks noblest, o'er the gathered kine
Preeminent: such glory in that hour
Gave Zeus to Agamemnon, to be first
And chiefest among hosts of mighty men.   515

   Now name me, Muses, ye that dwell in heaven—
For ye are goddesses, see all, all know;
We are but told a tale, and know not aught—
The captains and commanders of the Greeks.
I could not tell nor speak their multitude.   520
Had I ten tongues, ten mouths; were this my
       voice
Untiring, and the heart within me brass:—
But that those children of Olympus, sprung
Of Ægis-armèd Zeus, the Muses, know   524
Full well what numbers came 'neath Ilion's walls.
Now tell I all the captains, all the ships.

   Of the Bœotians Peneleus was chief,
Archesilaüs, Clonius, Leïtus,
And Prothoënor. Some in Hyria dwelt,
Schœnus or stony Aulis, or the dells   530
Of Eteonus: in Thespeia some,
Scholus and Graia, and the broad champaign
Of Mycalessus, Harma, Eilesius,
Erythræ, Eleon, Hyle, Peneon,

Ochaleæ, and Medeon, well-walled town,   535
Copæ, Eutresis, and the haunt of doves
Thisbè.   In Coroneia, on the lawns
Of Haliartus: by Plataia, by
Glisas, and Hypothebæ, well-walled town:
Onchestus, or Poseidon's holy grove,   540
Mideia, Arnè, where the grapes grow thick,
Or sacred Cilla, or the frontier-town
Anthedon.   Fifty ships went forth of these.
A hundred men and twenty sailed in each.

They of Aspledon and Orchomenos   545
Obeyed Ascalaphus and Ialmenus,
Chiefs whom in Actor's palace, Azeus' son,
The young Astyochè to Ares bore,
Her secret bridegroom, in her maiden's tower.
Full thirty chiselled ships did these array.   550

Of Phocians Schedius and Epistrophus
Ranked foremost, sons of proud Iphitus, son
Of Nauboleus.   Of Cyparissus these
Were lords, and stony Python, Crisa's grove,
Daulis and Panopeus; dwelt round about   555
Anemoreia and Hyampolis,
Or drank of holiest Cephissus' stream,
Or held Lilaia, whence Cephissus springs.
And forty dark ships were their retinue.

These two were captains of the Phocian lines, 560
Next the Bœotians ranging, on the left.

    The Locrian's prince, fleet Aias, Oileus' son,
Slighter than Aias son of Telamon,
Far slighter—small and linen-corsleted— 564
Yet with the spear surpassed the hosts of Greece.
From Cynus, Opöeis, Calliarus, these,
Bessa or Scarphè, sweet Augeæ came,
Thronius, or Tarphè by Boagrius' stream.
Forty dark ships were theirs, who o'er against
The great Eubœa dwelt—the Locrians. 570

    Eubœa's hosts, the Abantians—men whose lips
Breathe war—from Chalcis, Histiaia's vines,
Cerinthus' sands, Eirethria, Dion's steep,
Or Styra or Carystus: that proud race
Brave Elephenor led, Chalcodon's son. 575
He led the fleet Abantians: warriors, shorn
Of their front locks; with outstretched spears athirst
To rive the breastplate on the foeman's breast.
Forty dark vessels followed in his wake.

    And they who dwelt in Athens, well-walled town, 580
Land of great-souled Erechtheus—whom in days

Gone by the child of Zeus, Athenè, reared
(From bounteous Earth he sprang,) and bade him
    dwell
In Athens, in her own rich sanctuary:
There do Athenian warriors worship him,   585
As years roll round, with bullocks and with
    rams—
Their captain was Menestheus, Peteos' son.
In all the earth his like hath not arisen
To marshal steeds and shielded infantry.   589
Nestor alone might match him: Nestor's years
Were more.—And fifty dark ships followed him.

  Next, Aias brought twelve ships from Salamis;
And moored them by the Athenian phalanxes.

  And them whom Argos reared; from Tiryns'
    walls,
Hermionè and Asinè—that front   595
Each a deep bay—from Trœzen, Eïon,
And vine-clad Epidaurus: all who came
From Mases or Ægina, men of war:
Loud Diomedes ruled, and Sthenelus,
Famed Capaneus's son: Euryalus third,   600
His sire Mecisteus, *his* Talaïon.
Loud Diomedes ruled the whole array,
In eighty dark ships mustering.

                    Those who held
Mycenæ or Cleonæ, well-walled towns,   605
Or sumptuous Corinth, Araithyria sweet,
Orneia, or where first Adrastus reigned,
Sicyon; who dwelt on Gonoessa's steep,
Or Hyperesia; by Pellenè dwelt
And Ægius, and all along the coast,   610
And round broad Helicè: their hundred ships
Were led by Agamemnon Atreus' son.
Most noble as most numerous were the hosts
That followed him. Amongst them he stood armed
In dazzling brass, exulting: and of all   615
The mighty men stood chiefest, as of all
Noblest was he, and most his following.

   And those who tilled Laconia's rugged dales,
Pharis or Sparta, or the haunt of doves
Messè; Amyclæ, Helos' sea-washed walls,   620
Laäs or Œtylus: Menelaüs led,
The king's own brother, of the ringing voice,
Full fifty ships. They mixed not with the rest.
He moved amongst them, trusting in his might,
And urged to battle: this his heart's desire, 625
That Helen's tears and anguish be avenged.

   And those from Pylos, from Arenè fair,
Thrios, the ford of Alpheus, Æpy's walls,

Cyparisseïs, Helos, Pteleon,
Amphigeneia, Dorion :—where the Nine   630
Fell in with Thracian Thamyris, on his road
From Thessaly, the home of Eurytus,
And silenced all his songs : because he stood
Their vaunted conqueror, would they but appear—
Those Muses, sprung of Ægis-armèd Zeus—   635
And sing against him : they, thereat enraged,
Smote him with blindness, took away that gift
Divine, that he forgat his minstrelsy :—
Their chief was Nestor, the Gerenian knight.
And ninety chiselled ships were their array.   640

Them of Arcadia, 'neath Cyllenè's steep,
By Æpytus's tomb, where dwells a race
Of wrestlers : them of Rhipæ, Pheneüs,
Orchomenos white with sheep, and Stratia,
Wind-swept Enispè, fair Mantinea,   645
Tegea, Stymphelus, and Parrhasia :—
King Agapenor led, Anchæus' son.
Their ships were sixty : each ship furnished well
With men inured to war, Arcadia's sons.
To these did Agamemnon, King of men—   650
For they were landsmen—give of his own store
Ships and good oars, to cross the purple seas.

They of Buprasium and great Elis ; all

Whom utmost Myrsinus, Olenia's crags,
Hyrminè and Aleisium compass round ; 655
These had four chiefs—on each chief war-ships ten
Attended, with Epeans freighted well.
Part did Amphimachus, part Thalpius lead,
(Sprung, this from Cteatus, that from Eurytus
The seed of Actor ;) stout Diorès part 660
Whose sire was Amarynceus : o'er the fourth
Ruled brave Polyxenus—his sire the king
Agasthenes, who sprang from Ægeus' loins.

Them of Dulichium, and the sacred isles
That fronting Elis lie, beyond the sea, 665
The Echinæ : Meges marshalled, Phyleus' son,
In fight an Ares. Zeus loved well the knight
Phyleus his sire ; who with his grandsire wroth
Came down unto Dulichium long ago.
Forty dark vessels followed after him. 670

The Cephalenians, haughty race, and all
Who called the quivering woods of Neritos,
Or Ithaca, or rugged Ægilips,
Their home, or Crocylæa : all who dwelt
Round Samos or Zacynthus ; and whoe'er 675
Peopled, or faced, the mainland : these obeyed
Odysseus, like in counsel unto Zeus.
And with him sailed twelve scarlet-painted ships.

The Ætolians Thoas led, Andræmon's son;
By Pleuron, Olenus, Pylenè, reared,   680
Or Chalcis' beach, or rocky Calydon.
For Œneus' bold sons were not; he himself
Was not, nor fair-haired Meleager, now.
So o'er Ætolia's hosts supreme command
Held Thoas. Forty dark ships followed him.   685

Idomeneus, brave lance, the Cretans led.
From Cnosus and Miletus, Gortyn's walls,
And Lyttus, and Lycastus, glistening white,
Phæstus and Rhytius, peopled towns, they came,
And all the parts of hundred-citied Crete.   690
Idomeneus led those, and Meriones,
Match of the war-god, when he lift his arm
For slaughter. Eighty dark ships followed them.

Tlepolemus, the son of Heracles,
Valiant and tall, led on nine vessels, manned   695
By noble Rhodians, dwelling round about
Rhodes in three portions: in Ielysus,
And Lindus, and Cameirus glistening white.
These did Tlepolemus, brave lance, command:
Astyocheia bare him to the might   700
Of Heracles; who led the maid away
From Sella's stream, from Ephyrè, many a town
Of warriors, sons of heaven, laid first in dust.

He, grown to manhood in his stately home,
Slew straightway his sire's uncle, now in years, 705
Licymnius, sprung from Ares; built him ships
Forthwith, and fled, much people in his train,
O'er ocean; for he feared the other sons
And grandsons of the might of Heracles.
To Rhodes, much hardship past, the wanderer came:
There in three clans he settled; there obtained 711
The love of Zeus, whom heaven and earth obey.
Cronion's hand shed o'er them boundless wealth.

Nireus from Symè led three shapely ships:
Nireus, to Charopus and Aglaia born, 715
Nireus, of all the Greeks that came to Troy
The goodliest; all, save Peleus' noble son.
Yet poor his prowess, scant his following.

Them of Nisyrus, Crapathus, Casos, Cos,
Where reigned Eurypylus, and Calydnæ's isles, 720
Pheidippus led and Antiphus, two sons
Of Thessalus, who sprang from Heracles.
And thirty chiselled ships were their array.

Next, all who in Pelasgic Argos dwelt,
Whose home was Trachis, Alos, Alopè, 725
Phthia, and Hellas, for sweet damsels famed;—
Their fifty ships Achilles led to war:

Myrmidons, or Hellens, or Achaians hight.
Yet the dread din of battle woke not them:
For there was no man to array their hosts. 730
For in his ship their great swift leader lay,
Wroth for Briseis' sake, that fair-haired maid
Whom from Lyrnessus in hard fight he won,
When fell Lyrnessus and the walls of Thebes;
Epistrophus and Mynes, spearmen bold, 735
Smiting, Evenus' sons, of Sclepius' blood :—
For her sake lay he still—but not for long.

From Phylacè and flowery Pyrasus,
Demeter's own; from sheep-clad Iton some,
And sea-washed Antron, and green Pteleus, came.
Protesilaüs was their warrior chief 741
Once: but the dark soil was his lodging now.
In Phylacè his widow tore her cheeks,
Unfinished stood his home: for, first of Greeks
Leaping to land, a Dardan struck him down. 745
They mourned their chief, yet were not chiefless
 still:
Podarces led them, bred to warfare, son
Of rich Iphiclus, son of Phylacus;
Of proud Protesilaüs brother born:
But younger, and less brave, than that great
 chief 750
Protesilaüs. Leader lacked they not;

Yet thought, regretful, on the brave man dead.
Forty dark ships these manned.

      And those who tilled
Pheras by Lake Bœbeis, Glaphyræ,
Or Bœbè or Iolcos, well-walled town :   755
Admetus' son led their eleven ships,
Eumelus, whom Alcestis, lady fair,
Of Pelias' daughters loveliest, bare to him.

 Those whom Methonè, whom Thaumachia reared,
Or Melibœa, or Olizon's crags ;   760
Them Philoctetes led, an archer trained,
Seven ships : in each sat fifty rowers trained
Archers, in fight right valiant. But he lay,
Racked by strong pangs, in Lemnos' sacred isle,
Abandoned of the children of the Greeks 765
To rue the fell bite of the deadly snake.
There he lay sorrowing. But the Greeks were soon
To think of Philoctetes once again.
Chiefless they were not, though they mourned their
   chief.
Medon arrayed them, Rhenè's bastard child, 770
By city-sacking Oileus.

      Them who held
Œchalia, where Œchalian Eurytus

Was king, or Triccè, or Ithomè's rocks:
These Podaleirius and Machaon led,
Asclepius' two sons, of healing arts   775
Each master. Thirty chiselled ships ranged they.

Them from Ormenius, Hypereia's rill,
Asterius, and Titanus' white-faced cliffs;
Euæmon's glorious son, Eurypylus,
Led forth. And forty dark ships followed him. 780

Argissa's, Orthè's and Gyrtona's hosts,
White Olöessa's, and Elonè's ; led
The sturdy Polypœtes, son of him
Whom deathless Zeus begat, Peirithoüs.
Him to Peirithoüs famed Hippodamè   785
Bare, when those shaggy Beasts his vengeance
        felt,
From Pelion unto far-off Pindus driven.
Leonteus, bred to warfare, shared his toil,
Haughty Coronus' son, of Cæneus' blood.
And forty dark ships followed after these.   790

Gouneus from Cyphos twenty ships and two
Led. Enienians thronged them, and the men
Whose homes were round Dodona's storm-beat
        crags,
Sturdy Peræbians, or who tilled the meads

Of Titaresius, that pleasant stream   795
That flows in beauty down to Penëus;
Yet with that silver-eddied river ne'er
Mingleth, but oil-like, on the surface swims:
For Penëus is an arm of that oath-witness, Styx.

Prothoüs, Tenthredon's son, led Magnè's hosts,
By Penëus reared, and Pelion's quivering woods.
Forty dark ships of theirs swift Prothoüs led.   802

These were the chiefs and captains of the host.
Now, tell me, Muse, who far surpassed their mates,
Horsemen or steeds, in all that chivalry.   805

Of steeds the noblest far Eumelus drave,
Driv'n once by Pheres; swift in flight as birds,
In age, hue, depth of shoulder, fairly matched.
Those mares the Monarch of the Silver Bow
Bred in Pereia, couriers of dread war.   810
  Of men far first was Aias, Telamon's son,
While Peleus' son was wroth. For all unmatched
Was great Achilles, all unmatched his steeds.
But in his beaked sea-vessels wroth he lay
At Agamemnon, shepherd of the host.   815
His army by the breakers on the beach
With spear and quoit and bow made holiday:

While, ranged beside their several cars, their
    steeds
On lotus browsed and parsley of the lake.
Tented, in canvas, stood the chieftains' cars.   820
Reft of their warrior prince, they roamed at will
Among the host, and went not forth to war.

On came they: so might fire o'errun the lands.
Groaned earth beneath: as when Zeus smites in
    wrath,
Revelling in thunderstorm, the soil that hides   825
The Dragon, where in Arimi men shew
The Dragon's grave. Beneath their coming feet
Groaned she right sore. They swiftly scoured the
    plain.

And now wind-swift to Troy fleet Iris came
From Ægis-armèd Zeus, to tell a tale   830
Of woe. By Priam's gates assembled all
The assembly, young and old. Then, standing near,
Spake swift-foot Iris in Polites' voice,
Priam's son, who, trusting to his feats of speed,
High upon ancient Æsyætes' tomb   835

A spy sat watching till the Achaians moved
From shipboard.   So disguised, fleet Iris spake.

" Sire ! Thou aye lov'st entanglements of words.
Thus erst in peace-time : but 'tis stern war now.
Lo! I have looked on many a foughten field :   840
But ne'er saw yet so vast, so stout, a host,
As, even like the leaves or like the sand,
March o'er the plain, to fight beneath our walls.
But, Hector, be my message first to thee.
This do.   In Priam's great city many allies   845
Dwell, late o'er earth wide-scattered, and their speech
Is diverse.   Let each captain then command,
Each head, his own troops : marshalling first his hosts."

She spake. He knew her voice who spake to him.   849
And brake the assembly up. To arms they rushed.
The gates flew open, and the hosts poured forth,
Horsemen and footmen.   Mighty was their din.

Far in the plain, a steep hill fronts the walls;
A man may walk all round it : called by men
The Bramble-hill, but by the gods the tomb   855

Of supple-limbed Myrinè.   There were ranged
Both Trojans and allies.

       The Trojan host
Obeyed tall Hector of the glancing plume,
Priam's son. Most noble as most numerous shewed
His hosts: each spear-arm lusting for the fray. 860

Gallant Æneas led the Dardan lines;
Whom Aphroditè's self to Anchises bore
In Ida's glens; a goddess loved a man.
Archilochus and Acamas shared his toil,
Trained in all arts of war, Antenor's sons.   865

Seleia's dwellers, low at Ida's foot,
Rich Trojans, that drink dark Æsepus' stream,
These Pandarus led, Lycaon's brilliant son;
His very bow was great Apollo's gift.

From Adrasteia and Apæsus' realm,   870
Tereia's steep and Pityeia, came
Hosts by Adrastus and Amphius led
Of linen corslet, Merops' sons, who ruled
Percotè. He, a seer among the seers,
Had said, "My children, go not up to war."   875
Yet recked they not—drawn on by the dark Powers
  of Death.

Them who round Practium and Percotè dwelt,
Sestus, Abydos, and Arisbè's grove;
Ruled Asius, prince of warriors, Asius, son
Of Hyrtacus, whom vast and fiery-hued   880
Steeds from Arisbè brought, from Sella's stream.

The fierce Pelasgian spearmen — tribes who ploughed
Larissa's rich domain—Hippothoüs led:
Hippothoüs and Pylæus, warriors, sprung
Through Lethus from Pelasgian Teutamus.   885

Peiroüs and Acamas, mighty men, from Thrace,
Led all whom Hellespont, strong-rushing, belts.
Euphemus all Ciconia's spears: his sire
Trœzenus, son of Ceas, son of heaven.   889

Then the Pæonians, them who bend the bow,
From far-off Amydon Pyræcmes brought,
From Axius: Axius, whose vast-volumed tide,
Matchless in beauty, broadens o'er the lands.

The hairy bulk of stout Pylæmenes
The Paphlagonians roused from Eneti,   895
That breeds wild mules: Cytorus, Sesamos,
Their fair homes: Cromna or Parthenia's banks,
Ægialus, or Erythinæ tall.

Odius, Epistrophus, Calydon's hosts
Led from far Alybæ.   There is silver found.   900

The Mysians Cromis led, and Ennomus
The augur.   Not by augury to escape
Black death.   By fleet Achilles' hand he died
In Xanthus.   Other Trojans fell that day.

Godlike Ascanius led, and Phorcys, troops   905
From far Ascania; Phrygians, war-athirst.
Mæonians, Antiphus and Mesthles, born
By Lake Gygeis to Talaimenes.
They led Mæonians, born at Tmolus' foot.

The barbarous-talking Carians Nastes led,   910
These held Miletus, and Mæander's stream,
And rocky Phtheiræ's leaf-entangled shades,
And Mycalè's steep heights.   Amphimachus
Led these, and Nastes, Nomion's brilliant sons,
Amphimachus and Nastes.   Gold he had;   915
Yet, child-like, went to war.   Poor fool! what shield
Is gold against the bitterness of death?
He too must die by fleet Achilles' hand
In Xanthus.   Brave Achilles took his gold.

Sarpedon and good Glaucus Lycians led   920
From Lycia far, where whirls Scamander's stream.

FROM ILIAD I.

IN HEXAMETERS.

SING, O daughter of heaven, of Peleus' son, of Achilles,
Him whose terrible wrath brought thousand woes on Achaia.
Many a stalwart soul did it hurl untimely to Hades,
Souls of the heroes of old: and their bones lay strown on the sea-sands,
Prey to the vulture and dog. Yet was Zeus fulfilling a purpose;
Since that far-off day, when in hot strife parted asunder
Atreus' sceptred son, and the chos'n of heaven, Achilles.
  Say then, which of the Gods bid arise up battle between them?
Zeus's and Leto's son. With the king was kindled his anger:
Then went sickness abroad, and the people died of the sickness: 10

For that of Atreus' son had his priest been lightly entreated,
Chryses, Apollo's priest. For he came to the ships of Achaia,
Bearing a daughter's ransom, a sum not easy to number:
And in his hand was the emblem of Him, far-darting Apollo,
High on a sceptre of gold: and he prayed to the hosts of Achaia;
Chiefly to Atreus' sons, twin chieftains, ordering armies.
 "Chiefs sprung of Atreus' loins; and ye, brazen-greavèd Achaians!
So may the Gods this day, the Olympus-palacèd, grant you
Priam's city to raze, and return unscathed to your homesteads:
Only my own dear daughter I ask; take ransom and yield her, 20
Rev'rencing His great name, son of Zeus, far-darting Apollo."
 Then from the host of Achaians arose tumultuous answer:
"Due to the priest is his honour; accept rich ransom and yield her."
But there was war in the spirit of Atreus' son, Agamemnon;

Disdainful he dismissed him, a right stern fiat
    appending :—
"Woe be to thee, old man, if I find thee linger-
    ing longer,
Yea or returning again, by the hollow ships of
    Achaians!
Scarce much then will avail thee the great god's
    sceptre and emblem.
Her will I never release. Old age must first come
    upon her,
In my own home, yea in Argos, afar from the land
    of her fathers,   30
Following the loom, and attending upon my bed.
    But avaunt thee!
Go, and provoke not me, that thy way may be haply
    securer."

  These were the words of the king, and the old
    man feared and obeyed him:
Voiceless he went by the shore of the great dull-
    echoing ocean,
Thither he gat him apart, that ancient man; and a
    long prayer
Prayed to Apollo his Lord, son of golden-ringleted
    Leto:
  "Lord of the silver bow, thou whose arm girds
    Chryse and Cilla,—
Cilla beloved of the Gods,—and in might sways
    Tenedos, hearken!

Oh! if, in days gone by, I have built from floor unto
    cornice,
Smintheus, a fair shrine for thee; or burned in the
    flames of the altar   40
Fat flesh of bulls and of goats; then do this thing
    that I ask thee;
Hurl on the Greeks thy shafts, that thy servant's
    tears be avengèd!"
  So did he pray, and his prayer reached the ears
    of Phœbus Apollo.
Dark was the soul of the god as he moved from the
    heights of Olympus,
Shouldering a bow, and a quiver on this side fast
    and on that side.
Onward in anger he moved. And the arrows,
    stirred by the motion,
Rattled and rang on his shoulder: he came as
    cometh the midnight.
Hard by the ships he stayed him, and loosed one
    shaft from the bow-string;
Harshly the stretched string twanged of the bow all
    silvery-shining.
First fell his wrath on the mules, and the swift-
    footed hound of the herdsman;   50
Afterward smote he the host. With a rankling
    arrow he smote them
Aye; and the morn and the even were red with the
    glare of the corpse-fires.

Nine days over the host sped the shafts of the
    god : and the tenth day
Dawned ; and Achilles said, " Be a council called of
    the people."
(Such thought came to his mind from the goddess,
    Hera the white-armed,
Hera who loved those Greeks, and who saw them
    dying around her.)
So when all were collected and ranged in a solemn
    assembly,
Straightway rose up amidst them and spake swift-
    footed Achilles :—

"Atreus' son ! it were better, I think this day,
    that we wandered
Back, re-seeking our homes, (if a warfare *may* be
    avoided) ;   60
Now when the sword and the plague, these two
    things, fight with Achaians.
Come, let us seek out now some priest, some seer
    amongst us,
Yea or a dreamer of dreams—for a dream too
    cometh of God's hand—
Whence we may learn what hath angered in this
    wise Phœbus Apollo.
Whether mayhap he reprove us of prayer or of oxen
    unoffered ;
Whether, accepting the incense of lambs and of
    blemishless he-goats,

Yet it be his high will to remove this misery from us."

Down sat the prince: he had spoken. And up-rose to them in answer
Kalchas Thestor's son, high chief of the host of the augurs.
Well he knew what is present, what will be, and what was aforetime: 70
He into Ilion's harbour had led those ships of Achaia,
All by the power of the Art, which he gained from Phœbus Apollo.
Thus then, kindliest-hearted, arising spake he before them:
"Peleus' son! Thou demandest, a man heaven-favour'd, an answer
Touching the Great King's wrath, the afar-off-aiming Apollo:
Therefore I lift up my voice. Swear thou to me, duly digesting
All,—that with right good will, by word and by deed, thou wilt aid me.
Surely the ire will awaken of one who mightily ruleth
Over the Argives all: and upon him wait the Achaians.
Aye is the battle the king's, when the poor man kindleth his anger: 80

For, if but this one day he devour his indig-
nation,
Still on the morrow abideth a rage, that its end be
accomplished,
Deep in the soul of the king. So bethink thee,
wilt thou deliver."

Then unto him making answer arose swift-footed
Achilles:
" Fearing naught, up and open the god's will, all
that is told thee:
For by Apollo's self, heaven's favourite, whom thou,
Kalchas,
Serving aright, to the armies aloud God's oracles
op'nest:
None—while as yet I breathe upon earth, yet walk
in the daylight—
Shall, at the hollow ships, lift hand of oppression
against thee,
None out of all your host—not and if thou nam'st
Agamemnon, 90
Who now sits in his glory, the topmost flower of the
armies."

Then did the blameless prophet at last take
courage and answer:
" Lo ! He doth not reprove us of prayer or of oxen
unoffered;
But for his servant's sake, the disdained of king
Agamemnon,

(In that he loosed not his daughter, inclined not his
　　　ear to a ransom,)
Therefore the Far-darter sendeth, and yet shall send
　　　on us, evil.
Nor shall he stay from the slaughter the hand that
　　　is heavy upon you,
Till to her own dear father the bright-eyed maiden
　　　is yielded,
No price asked, no ransom ; and ships bear hallowèd
　　　oxen
Chryse-wards :—then, it may be, will he shew mercy
　　　and hear us." 100
　These words said, sat he down. Then rose in
　　　his place and addressed them
Atreus' warrior son, Agamemnon king of the
　　　nations,
Sore grieved. Fury was working in each dark cell
　　　of his bosom,
And in his eye was a glare as a burning fiery fur-
　　　nace :
First to the priest he addressed him, his whole mien
　　　boding a mischief.
　" Priest of ill luck ! Never heard I of aught good
　　　from thee, but evil.
Still doth the evil thing unto thee seem sweeter of
　　　utt'rance ;
Leaving the thing which is good all unspoke, all
　　　unaccomplished.

Lo! this day to the people thou say'st, God's
 oracles op'ning,
What, but that *I* am the cause why the god's hand
 worketh against them,   110
For that in sooth I rejected a ransom, ay and a rich
 one,
Brought for the girl Briseis. I did. For I chose
 to possess her,
Rather, at home: less favour hath Clytemnestra be-
 fore me,
Clytemnestra my wife: unto her Briseis is equal,
Equal in form and in stature, in mind and in
 womanly wisdom.
Still, even thus, am I ready to yield her, so it be
 better:
Better is saving alive, I hold, than slaying a nation.
Meanwhile deck me a guerdon in her stead, lest of
 Achaians
I should alone lack honour; an unmeet thing and a
 shameful.
See all men, that my guerdon, I wot not whither it
 goeth."   120
  Then unto him made answer the swift-foot chief-
 tain Achilles:
"O most vaunting of men, most gain-loving, off-
 spring of Atreus!
How shall the lords of Achaia bestow fresh guerdon
 upon thee?

Surely we know not yet of a treasure piled in abundance!
That which the sacking of cities hath brought to us, all hath an owner,
Yea it were all unfit that the host make redistribution.
Yield thou the maid to the god. So threefold surely and fourfold
All we Greeks will requite thee, should that day dawn, when the great gods
Grant that of yon proud walls not one stone rest on another."

* * * * *

VIRGIL'S ECLOGUES.

G

VIRGIL'S ECLOGUES.

ECLOGUE I.

MELIBŒUS. TITYRUS.

M.

STRETCHED in the shadow of the broad beech, thou
    Rehearsest, Tityrus, on the slender pipe
    Thy woodland music. We our fatherland
    Are leaving, we must shun the fields we love:
    While, Tityrus, thou, at ease amid the shade,
    Bidd'st answering woods call Amaryllis 'fair.'

T.   O Melibœus! 'Tis a god that made
    For me this holiday: for god I'll aye
    Account him; many a young lamb from my fold
    Shall stain his altar. Thanks to him, my kine 10
    Range, as thou seest them: thanks to him, I play
    What songs I list upon my shepherd's pipe.

M.   For me, I grudge thee not; I marvel much:
    So sore a trouble is in all the land.
    Lo! feeble *I* am driving hence my goats—

Nay *dragging*, Tityrus, one, and that with pain.
For, yeaning here amidst the hazel-stems,
She left her twin kids—on the naked flint
She left them; and I lost my promised flock.
This evil, I remember, oftentimes,   20
(Had not my wits been wandering,) oaks fore-
  told
By heaven's hand smitten: oft the wicked crow
Croaked the same message from the rifted
  holm.
—Yet tell me, Tityrus, of this 'God' of thine.

T. The city men call *Rome* my folly deemed
Was e'en like this of ours, where week by week
We shepherds journey with our weanling flocks.
So whelp to dog, so kid (I knew) to dam
Was likest: and I judged great things by
  small.
But o'er all cities this so lifts her head,   30
As doth o'er osiers lithe the cypress tree.

M. What made thee then so keen to look on Rome?

T. Freedom: who marked, at last, my helpless
  state:
Now that a whiter beard than that of yore
Fell from my razor: still she marked, and
  came
(All late) to help me—now that all my thought
Is Amaryllis, Galatea gone.

> While Galatea's, I despaired, I own,
> Of freedom, and of thrift. Though from my farm
> Full many a victim stept, though rich the cheese 40
> Pressed for yon thankless city: still my hand
> Returned not, heavy with brass pieces, home.

M. I wondered, Amaryllis, whence that woe,
> And those appeals to heav'n: for whom the peach
> Hung undisturbed upon the parent tree
> Tityrus was gone! Why, Tityrus, pine and rill,
> And all these copses, cried to thee, "Come home!"

T. What could I do? I could not step from out
> My bonds; nor meet, save there, with Pow'rs so kind.
> There, Melibœus, I beheld that youth 50
> For whom each year twelve days my altars smoke.
> Thus answered he my yet unanswered prayer;
> "Feed still, my lads, your kine, and yoke your bulls."

M. Happy old man! Thy lands are yet thine own!
> Lands broad enough for thee, although bare stones
> And marsh choke every field with reedy mud.

Strange pastures shall not vex thy teeming ewes,
Nor neighbouring flocks shed o'er them rank disease.
Happy old man! Here, by familiar streams
And holy springs, thou'lt catch the leafy cool. 60
Here, as of old, yon hedge, thy boundary line,
Its willow-buds a feast for Hybla's bees,
Shall with soft whisperings woo thee to thy sleep.
Here, 'neath the tall cliff, shall the vintager
Sing carols to the winds: while all the time
Thy pets, the stockdoves, and the turtles make
Incessantly their moan from aëry elms.

T. Aye, and for this shall slim stags graze in air,
And ocean cast on shore the shrinking fish;
For this, each realm by either wandered o'er,
Parthians shall Arar drink, or Tigris Gauls;
Ere from this memory shall fade that face! 72

M. And we the while must thirst on Libya's sands,
O'er Scythia roam, and where the Cretan stems
The swift Oaxes; or, with Britons, live
Shut out from all the world. Shall I e'er see,
In far-off years, my fatherland? the turf
That roofs my meagre hut? see, wondering last,
Those few scant cornblades that are realms to me?

What! must rude soldiers hold these fallows
   trim?   80
That corn barbarians? See what comes of strife,
Poor people—where we sowed, what hands
   shall reap!
Now, Melibœus, pr'ythee graft thy pears,
And range thy vines! Nay on, my she-goats, on,
Once happy flock! For never more must I,
Outstretched in some green hollow, watch you
   hang
From tufted crags, far up: no carols more
I'll sing: nor, shepherded by me, shall ye
Crop the tart willow and the clover-bloom.

T. Yet here, this one night, thou may'st rest
   with me,   90
Thy bed green branches. Chestnuts soft have I
And mealy apples, and our fill of cheese.
Already, see, the far-off chimneys smoke,
And deeper grow the shadows of the hills.

ECLOGUE II.

Corydon.

FOR one fair face—his master's idol—burned
   The shepherd Corydon; and hope had none.
Day after day he came ('twas all he could)

Where, piles of shadow, thick the beeches rose:
There, all alone, his unwrought phrases flung,
Bootless as passionate, to copse and crag.
 "Hardhearted! Naught car'st thou for all my songs,
Naught pitiest. I shall die, one day, for thee.
The very cattle court cool shadows now,
Now the green lizard hides beneath the thorn: 10
And for the reaper, faint with driving heat,
The handmaids mix the garlic-salad strong.
My only mates, the crickets—as I track
'Neath the fierce sun thy steps—make shrill the woods.
Better to endure the passion and the pride
Of Amaryllis: better to endure
Menalcas—dark albeit as thou art fair.
Put not, oh fair, in difference of hue
Faith overmuch: the white May-blossoms drop
And die; the hyacinth swart, men gather it. 20
Thy scorn am I: thou ask'st not whence I am,
How rich in snowy flocks, how stored with milk.
O'er Sicily's green hills a thousand lambs
Wander, all mine: my new milk fails me not
In summer or in snow. Then I can sing
All songs Amphion the Dircæan sang,
Piping his flocks from Attic Aracynth.
Nor am I all uncouth. For yesterday,

When winds had laid the seas, I, from the shore,
Beheld my image.   Little need I fear   30
Daphnis, though thou wert judge, or mirrors lie.
—Oh! be content to haunt ungentle fields,
A cottager, with me; bring down the stag,
And with green switch drive home thy flocks of kids:
Like mine, thy woodland songs shall rival Pan's!
—'Twas Pan first taught us reed on reed to fit
With wax: Pan watches herd and herdsman too.
—Nor blush that reeds should chafe thy pretty lip.
What pains Amyntas took, this skill to gain!
I have a pipe—seven stalks of different lengths   40
Compose it—which Damœtas gave me once.
Dying he said, "At last 'tis all thine own."
The fool Amyntas heard, and grudged, the praise.
Two fawns moreover (perilous was the gorge
Down which I tracked them!)—dappled still each
    skin—
Drain daily two ewe-udders; all for thee.
Long Thestylis has cried to make them hers.
Hers be they—since to thee my gifts are dross.

Be mine, oh fairest!   See! for thee the Nymphs
Bear baskets lily-laden: Naiads bright   50
For thee crop poppy-crests and violets pale,
With daffodil and fragrant fennel-bloom:
Then, weaving casia in and all sweet things,

Soft hyacinth paint with yellow marigold.
Apples *I*'ll bring thee, hoar with tender bloom,
And chestnuts—which my Amaryllis loved,
And waxen plums: let plums too have their day.
And thee I'll pluck, oh bay, and, myrtle, thee
Its neighbour: neighboured thus your sweets shall
      mix.
—Pooh! Thou 'rt a yokel, Corydon. Thy love   60
Laughs at thy gifts: if gifts must win the day,
Rich is Iolas. What thing have I,
Poor I, been asking—while the winds and boars
Ran riot in my pools and o'er my flowers?

—Yet, fool, whom fliest thou? Gods have dwelt in
      woods,
And Dardan Paris. Citadels let her
Who built them, Pallas, haunt: green woods for me.
Grim lions hunt the wolf, and wolves the kid,
And kids at play the clover-bloom. I hunt
Thee only: each one drawn to what he loves.   70
See! trailing from their necks the kine bring home
The plough, and, as he sinks, the sun draws out
To twice their length the shadows. Still I burn
With love. For what can end or alter love?

Thou 'rt raving, simply raving, Corydon.
Clings to thy leafy elm thy half-pruned vine.

Why not begin, at least, to plait with twigs
And limber reeds some useful homely thing?
Thou 'lt find another love, if scorned by this.

ECLOGUE III.

Menalcas. Damœtas. Palæmon.

M.

W̲HOSE flock, Damœtas? Melibœus's?
    D. No, Ægon's. Ægon left it in my care.
M. Unluckiest of flocks! Your master courts
    Neæra, wondering if she like me more:
    Meanwhile a stranger milks you twice an hour,
    Saps the flocks' strength, and robs the suckling
      lambs.
D. Yet fling more charily such words at *men*.
    You—while the goats looked goatish—we
      know who,
    And in what chapel—(but the kind Nymphs
      laughed)—
M. Then (was it?) when they saw me Micon's
    shrubs   10
    And young vines hacking with my rascally
      knife?

D. Or when by this old beech you broke the bow
And shafts of Daphnis: which you cried to see,
You crossgrained lad, first given to the boy;
And harm him somehow you must needs, or die.
M. Where will lords stop, when knaves are come to this?
Did not I see you, scoundrel, in a snare
Take Damon's goat, Wolf barking all the while?
And when I shouted, "Where's he off to? Call,
Tityrus, your flock,"—you skulked behind the sedge. 20
D. Beaten in singing, should he have withheld
The goat my pipe had by its music earned?
That goat was mine, you mayn't p'r'aps know: and he
Owned it himself; but said he could not pay.
M. He beat by you? You own a decent pipe?
Used you not, dunce, to stand at the crossroads,
Stifling some lean tune in a squeaky straw?
D. Shall we then try in turn what each can do?
I stake yon cow—nay hang not back—she comes
Twice daily to the pail, is suckling twins. 30
Say what *you*'ll lay.
M.   I durst not wager aught
Against you from the flock: for I have at home
A father, I have a tyrant stepmother.

Both count the flock twice daily, one the kids.
But what *you*'ll own far handsomer, I'll stake
(Since you will be so mad) two beechen cups,
The carved work of the great Alcimedon.
O'er them the chiseller's skill has traced a vine
That drapes with ivy pale her wide-flung curls.
Two figures in the centre: Conon one, 40
And—what's that other's name, who'd take a wand
And shew the nations how the year goes round;
When you should reap, when stoop behind the plough?
Ne'er yet my lips came near them, safe hid up.

D. For *me* two cups the selfsame workman made,
And clasped with lissom briar the handles round.
Orpheus i' the centre, with the woods behind.
Ne'er yet my lips came near them, safe hid up.
—This talk of cups, if on my cow you've fixed
Your eye, is idle.

M. Nay you'll not this day 50
Escape me. Name your spot, and I'll be there.
Our umpire be—Palæmon; here he comes!
I'll teach you how to challenge folks to sing.

D. Come on, if aught is in you. I'm not loth,
I shrink from no man. Only, neighbour, thou
('Tis no small matter) lay this well to heart.

P. Say on, since now we sit on softest grass;
And now buds every field and every tree,
And woods are green, and passing fair the year.
Damœtas, lead. Menalcas, follow next. 60
Sing verse for verse: such songs the Muses love.

D. With Jove we open. Jove fills everything,
He walks the earth, he listens when I sing.
M. Me Phœbus loves. I still have offerings meet
For Phœbus; bay, and hyacinth blushing sweet.
D. Me Galatea pelts with fruit, and flies
(Wild girl) to the woods: but first would catch my eyes.
M. Unbid Amyntas comes to me, my flame;
With Delia's self my dogs are not more tame.
D. Gifts have I for my fair: who marked but I 70
The place where doves had built their nest sky-high?
M. I've sent my poor gift, which the wild wood bore,
Ten golden apples. Soon I'll send ten more.
D. Oft Galatea tells me—what sweet tales!
Waft to the god's ears just a part, ye gales.
M. At heart Amyntas loves me. Yet what then?
He mates with hunters, I with servingmen.
D. Send me thy Phyllis, good Iolas, now.
Today's my birthday. When I slay my cow

	To help my harvest—come, and welcome, thou. 80
M.	Phillis is *my* love. When we part, she'll cry; And fain would bid Iolas' self good bye.[1]
D.	Wolves kill the flocks, and storms the ripened corn; And winds the tree; and me a maiden's scorn.
M.	Rain is the land's delight, weaned kids' the vine; Big ewes' lithe willow; and one fair face mine.
D.	Pollio loves well this homely muse of mine. For a new votary fat a calf, ye Nine. 88
M.	Pollio *makes* songs. For him a bull demand, Who butts, whose hoofs already spurn the sand.
D.	Who loves thee, Pollio, go where thou art gone. For him flow honey, thorns sprout cinnamon.
M.	Who loathes not Bavius, let him love thy notes, Mævius:—and yoke the fox, and milk he-goats.
D.	Flowers and ground-strawberries while your prize ye make,

---

[1] Putting the vocative "Iolla" in line 79, as Mr. Kennedy does, into the mouth of Menalcas, not of Phyllis, I would substitute these lines for my original ones:—

> Phillis is *my* dear love. She wept when I—
> (Yes I, Iollas,)—left her: and "Good-bye",
> She said, "Iollas fair; a long Good-bye".

  Cold in the grass—fly hence, lads—lurks the
   snake.
M. Sheep, banks are treacherous: draw not over-
   nigh:
  See, now the lordly ram his fleece doth dry.
D. Tityrus, yon she-goats from the river bring.
  I in due time will wash them at the spring. 100
M. Call, lads, your sheep. Once more our hands,
   should heat
  O'ertake the milk, will press in vain the teat.
D. How rich these vetches, yet how lean my ox.
  Love kills alike the herdsman and the flocks.
M. *My* lambs—and here love's not in fault, you'll
   own—
  Witched by some jealous eye, are skin and bone.
D. Say in what land—and great Apollo be
  To me—heaven's arch extends just cubits three.
M. Say in what lands with kings' names grav'n
   are grown
  Flowers—and be Phyllis yours and yours
   alone.   110
P. Not mine such strife to settle. You have earned
  A cow, and you: and whoso else shall e'er
  Shrink from love's sweets or prove his bitter-
   ness.
  Close, lads, the springs. The meads have
   drunk enough.

ECLOGUE IV.

MUSES of Sicily, a loftier song
Wake we! Some tire of shrubs and myrtles low.
Are woods our theme? Then princely be the woods.

Come are those last days that the Sybil sang:
The ages' mighty march begins anew.
Now comes the virgin, Saturn reigns again:
Now from high heaven descends a wondrous race.
Thou on the newborn babe—who first shall end
That age of iron, bid a golden dawn
Upon the broad world—chaste Lucina, smile: 10
Now thy Apollo reigns.   And, Pollio, thou
Shalt be our Prince, when he that grander age
Opens, and onward roll the mighty moons:
Thou, trampling out what prints our crimes have left,
Shalt free the nations from perpetual fear.
While he to bliss shall waken; with the Blest
See the Brave mingling, and be seen of them,
Ruling that world o'er which his father's arm shed
   peace.—

On thee, child, everywhere shall earth, untilled,
Show'r, her first baby-offerings, vagrant stems   20
Of ivy, foxglove, and gay briar, and bean;
Unbid the goats shall come big-uddered home,
Nor monstrous lions scare the herded kine.
Thy cradle shall be full of pretty flowers:
Die must the serpent, treacherous poison-plants
Must die; and Syria's roses spring like weeds.

But, soon as thou canst read of hero-deeds
Such as thy father wrought, and understand
What is true worth: the champaign day by day
Shall grow more yellow with the waving corn;   30
From the wild bramble purpling then shall hang
The grape; and stubborn oaks drop honeydew.
Yet traces of that guile of elder days
Shall linger; bidding men tempt seas in ships,
Gird towns with walls, cleave furrows in the land.
Then a new Tiphys shall arise, to man
New argosies with heroes: then shall be
New wars; and once more shall be bound for Troy,
A mightier Achilles.
     After this,
When thou hast grown and strengthened into
  man,
The pilot's self shall range the seas no more;   41
Nor, each land teeming with the wealth of all,

The floating pines exchange their merchandise.
Vines shall not need the pruning-hook, nor earth
The harrow: ploughmen shall unyoke their steers.
Nor then need wool be taught to counterfeit
This hue and that. At will the meadow ram
Shall change to saffron, or the gorgeous tints
Of Tyre, his fair fleece; and the grazing lamb
At will put crimson on.
     So grand an age 50
Did those three Sisters bid their spindles spin;
Three, telling with one voice the changeless will of
  Fate.

Oh draw—the time is all but present—near
To thy great glory, cherished child of heaven,
Jove's mighty progeny! And lo! the world,
The round and ponderous world, bows down to thee;
The earth, the ocean-tracts, the depths of heaven.
Lo! nature revels in the coming age.
Oh! may the evening of my days last on,
May breath be mine, till I have told thy deeds! 60
Not Orpheus then, not Linus, shall outsing
Me: though each vaunts his mother or his sire,
Calliopea this, Apollo that.
Let Pan strive with me, Arcady his judge;
Pan, Arcady his judge, shall yield the palm.

Learn, tiny babe, to read a mother's smile :
Already ten long months have wearied her.
Learn, tiny babe. Him, who ne'er knew such smiles,
Nor god nor goddess bids to board or bed.

ECLOGUE V.

Menalcas. Mopsus.

Me.

MOPSUS, suppose, now two good men have met—
   You at flute-blowing, as at verses I—
   We sit down here, where elm and hazel mix.
Mo. Menalcas, meet it is that I obey
   Mine elder. Lead, or into shade—that shifts
   At the wind's fancy—or (mayhap the best)
   Into some cave. See here's a cave, o'er which
   A wild vine flings her flimsy foliage.   8
Me. On these hills one—Amyntas—vies with you.
Mo. Suppose he thought to outsing Phœbus' self?
Me. Mopsus, begin. If aught you know of flames
   That Phyllis kindles; aught of Alcon's worth,
   Or Codrus's ill-temper; then begin:

Tityrus meanwhile will watch the grazing kids.
Mo.   Ay, I will sing the song which t'other day
On a green beech's bark I cut; and scored
The music, as I wrote. Hear that, and bid
Amyntas vie with me.
Me.   As willow lithe
Yields to pale olive; as to crimson beds
Of roses yields the lowly lavender;   20
So, to my mind, Amyntas yields to you.
Mo.   But, lad, no more: we are within the cave.

(*Sings.*) The Nymphs wept Daphnis, slain by ruthless death.
Ye, streams and hazels, were their witnesses:
When, clasping tight her son's unhappy corpse,
"Ruthless," the mother cried, " are gods and stars."
None to the cool brooks led in all those days,
Daphnis, his fed flocks: no four-footed thing
Stooped to the pool, or cropped the meadow-grass.   29
How lions of the desert mourned thy death,
Forests and mountains wild proclaim aloud.
'Twas Daphnis taught mankind to yoke in cars
The tiger; lead the winegod's revel on,
And round the tough spear twine the bending leaf.

Vines are the green wood's glory, grapes the
   vine's:
The bull the cattle's, and the rich land's corn
Thou art thy people's. When thou metst thy
   doom,
Both Pales and Apollo left our fields.
In furrows where we dropped big barley seeds,
Spring now rank darnel and the barren reed:
Not violet soft and shining daffodil,   41
But thistles rear themselves and sharp-spiked
   thorn.
Shepherds, strow earth with leaves, and hang
   the springs
With darkness! Daphnis asks of you such
   rites:
And raise a tomb, and place this rhyme thereon:
"Famed in the green woods, famed beyond
   the skies,
A fair flock's fairer lord, here Daphnis lies."

Me. Welcome thy song to me, oh sacred bard,
As, to the weary, sleep upon the grass:
As, in the summer-heat, a bubbling spring 50
Of sweetest water, that shall slake our thirst.
In song, as on the pipe, thy master's match,
Thou, gifted lad, shalt now our master be.
Yet will I sing in turn, in my poor way,

My song, and raise thy Daphnis to the stars—
Raise Daphnis to the stars. He loved me too.
Mo. Could aught in my eyes such a boon outweigh?
Song-worthy was thy theme: and Stimichon
Told me long since of that same lay of thine.
Me. (*Sings.*) Heaven's unfamiliar floor, and clouds and stars, 60
Fair Daphnis, wondering, sees beneath his feet.
Therefore gay revelries fill wood and field,
Pan, and the shepherds, and the Dryad maids.
Wolves plot not harm to sheep, nor nets to deer;
Because kind Daphnis makes it holiday.
The unshorn mountains fling their jubilant voice
Up to the stars: the crags and copses shout
Aloud, " A god, Menalcas, lo! a god."
Oh! be thou kind and good unto thine own!
Behold four altars, Daphnis: two for thee, 70
Two, piled for Phœbus. Thereupon I'll place
Two cups, with new milk foaming, year by year;
Two goblets filled with richest olive-oil:
And, first with much wine making glad the feast—
At the fireside in snowtime, 'neath the trees
In harvest—pour, rare nectar, from the can
The wines of Chios. Lyctian Ægon then

Shall sing me songs, and to Damœtas' pipe
Alphesibœus dance his Satyr-dance.
And this shalt thou lack never: when we pay
The Nymphs our vows, and when we cleanse
   the fields.   81
While boars haunt mountain-heights, and fishes
   streams,
Bees feed on thyme, and grasshoppers on dew,
Thy name, thy needs, thy glory shall abide.
As Bacchus and as Ceres, so shalt thou
Year after year the shepherd's vows receive;
So bind him to the letter of his vow.

Mo. What can I give thee, what, for such a song?
Less sweet to me the coming South-wind's sigh,
The sea-wave breaking on the shore, the noise
Of rivers, rushing through the stony vales. 91
Me. First I shall offer you this brittle pipe.
This taught me how to sing, "For one fair
   face:"
This taught me "Whose flock? Melibœus's?"
Mo. Take thou this crook; which oft Antigenes
Asked—and he then was loveable—in vain;
Brass-tipped and even-knotted—beautiful!

ECLOGUE VI.

MY muse first stooped to trifle, like the Greek's,
  In numbers; and, unblushing, dwelt in woods.
I sang embattled kings: but Cynthius plucked
My ear, and warned me: "Tityrus, fat should be
A shepherd's wethers, but his lays thin-drawn."
So—for enough and more will strive to tell,
Varus, thy deeds, and pile up grisly wars—
On pipe of straw will I my wood-notes sing:
I sing not all unbid. Yet oh! should one
Smit by great love, should one read this my lay— 10
Then with thee, Varus, shall our myrtle-groves,
And all these copses, ring. Right dearly loves
Phœbus the page that opens with thy name.

On, sisters!
         —Chromis and Mnasylus saw
(Two lads) Silenus in a cave asleep:
As usual, swoln with yesterday's debauch.
Just where it fell his garland lay hard by;
And on worn handle hung his ponderous can.
They—for the old man oft had cheated each
Of promised songs—draw near, and make his
    wreaths   20

Fetters to bind him.   Ægle makes a third,
(Ægle, the loveliest of the Naiad maids,)
To back their fears : and, as his eyes unclose,
Paints brow and temples red with mulberry.
He, laughing at the trick, cries, "Wherefore weave
These fetters ?   Lads, unbind me : 'tis enough
But to have seemed to have me in your power.
Ye ask a song ; then listen.   You I'll pay
With song : for her I've other meed in store."
And forthwith he begins.   Then might you see 30
Move to the music Faun and forest-beast,
And tall oaks bow their heads.   Not so delights
Parnassus in Apollo : not so charmed
At Orpheus Rhodope and Ismarus.

   For this he sang :—How, drawn from that vast
      void,
Gathered the germs of earth and air and sea
And liquid flame.   How the Beginning sprang
Thence, and the young world waxed into a ball.
Then Earth, grown harder, walled the sea-god off
In seas, and slowly took substantial form :   40
Till on an awed world dawned the wondrous sun,
And straight from heaven, by clouds unbroken, fell
The showers : as woods first bourgeoned, here and
      there
A wild beast wandering over hills unknown.

Of Pyrrha casting stones, and Saturn's reign,
The stolen fire, the eagles of the rock,
He sings: and then, beside what spring last seen
The sailors called for Hylas—till the shore
All rang with 'Hylas,' 'Hylas:'—and consoles
(Happy if horned herds never had been born,)   50
With some fair bullock's love Pasiphae.
Ah! hapless maid! What madness this of thine?
Once a king's daughters made believe to low,
And ranged the leas: but neither stooped to ask
Those base beasts' love: though each had often feared
To find the ploughman's gear about her neck,
And felt on her smooth brow for budding horns.
Ah! hapless maid! Thou roam'st from hill to hill:
He under some dark oak—his snowy side
Cushioned on hyacinths—chews the pale-green grass,   60
Or woos some favourite from the herd. "Close, Nymphs,
Dictæan Nymphs, oh close the forest-glades!
If a bull's random footprints by some chance
Should greet me! Lured, may be, by greener grass,
Or in the herd's wake following, vagrant kine
May bring him straight into my father's fold!"
—Then sings he of that maid who paused to gaze
At the charmed apples:—and surrounds with moss,

Bitter tree-moss, the daughters of the Sun,
Till up they spring tall alders.—Then he sings 70
How Gallus, wandering to Parnassus' stream,
A sister led to the Aonian hills,
And, in a mortal's honour, straight uprose
The choir of Phœbus: How that priest of song,
The shepherd Linus,—all his hair with flowers
And bitter parsley shining,—spake to him.
" Take—lo! the Muses give it thee—this pipe,
Once that Ascræan's old: to this would he
Sing till the sturdy mountain-ash came down.
Sing thou on this, whence sprang Æolia's grove, 80
Till in no wood Apollo glory more."

   So on and on he sang:—How Nisus, famed
In story, troubled the Dulichian ships;
And in the deep seas bid her sea-dogs rend
The trembling sailors. Tereus' tale he told,
How he was changed: what banquet Philomel,
What present, decked for him: and how she flew
To the far wilderness; and flying paused—
(Poor thing)—to flutter round her ancient home.

   All songs which one day Phœbus sang to
       charmed 90
Eurotas—and the laurels learnt them off—
He sang. The thrilled vales fling them to the stars
Till Hesper bade them house and count their flocks,
And journeyed all unwelcome up the sky.

ECLOGUE VII.

MELIBŒUS, CORYDON, THYRSIS.

M.

DAPHNIS was seated 'neath a murmurous oak,
When Corydon and Thyrsis (so it chanced)
Had driv'n their two flocks—one of sheep, and one
Of teeming goats—together: herdsmen both,
Both in life's spring, and able well to sing,
Or, challenged, to reply. To that same spot
I, guarding my young myrtles from the frost,
Find my goat strayed, the patriarch of the herd :
And straight spy Daphnis. He, espying me
In turn, cries, "Melibœus! hither, quick! 10
Thy goat, and kids, are safe. And if thou hast
An hour to spare, sit down beneath the shade.
Hither unbid will troop across the leas
The kine to drink : green Mincius fringes here
His banks with delicate bullrush, and a noise
Of wild bees rises from the sacred oak."

What could I do? Alcippe I had none,
Nor Phyllis, to shut up my new-weaned lambs:
Then, there was war on foot—a mighty war—
Thyrsis and Corydon!—So in the end   20
I made my business wait upon their sport.—
So singing verse for verse—that well the Muse
Might mark it—they began their singing-match.
Thus Corydon, thus Thyrsis sang in turn.
  (*They sing.*)

C. "Ye Fountain Nymphs, my loves! Grant me to sing
  Like Codrus:—next Apollo's rank his lines:—
Or here—if all may scarce do everything—
  I'll hang my pipe up on these sacred pines."

T. "Swains! a new minstrel deck with ivy now,
  Till Codrus burst with envy! Or, should he   30
Flatter o'ermuch, twine foxglove o'er my brow,
  Lest his knave's-flattery spoil the bard to be."

C. "'To Dian, from young Micon: this boar's head,
  And these broad antlers of a veteran buck.'
Full-length in marble—ancle-bound with red
  Buskins—I'll rear her, should to-day bring luck."

T. "Ask but this bowl, Priapus, and this cake
  Each year: for poor the garden thou dost keep.

  Our small means made thee marble: whom
   we'll make
    Of gold, should lambing multiply our
     sheep."   40

C. "Maid of the seas! more sweet than Hybla's
   thyme,
    Graceful as ivy, white as is the swan!
  When home the fed flocks wend at evening's
   prime,
    Then come—if aught thou car'st for Cory-
     don."

T. "Hark! bitterer than wormwood may I be,
    Bristling as broom, as drifted sea-weed cheap,
  If this day seem not a long year to me!
    Home, home for very shame, my o'er-fed
     sheep!"

C. "Ye mossy rills, and lawns more soft than
   dreams,   49
    Thinly roofed over by these leaves of green:
  From the great heat—now summer's come,
   now teems
    The jocund vine with buds—my cattle
     screen."

T. "Warm hearth, good faggots, and great fires
   you'll find
    In my home: black with smoke are all its
     planks:

> We laugh, who 're in it, at the chill north wind,
>> As wolves at troops of sheep, mad streams at banks."

C. "Here furry chestnuts rise and juniper:
>> Heaped 'neath each tree the fallen apples lie:
>
> All smiles. But, once let fair Alexis stir
>> From off these hills—and lo! the streams are dry." 60

T. "Thirsts in parched lands and dies the blighted grass;
>> Vines lend no shadow to the mountain-height;
>
> But groves shall bloom again, when comes my lass;
>> And in glad showers Jove descend in might."

C. "Poplars Alcides likes, and Bacchus vines;
>> Fair Venus myrtle, and Apollo bay;
>
> But while to hazel-leaves my love inclines,
>> Nor bays nor myrtles greater are than they."

T. "Fair in woods ash; and pine on garden-grass:
>> On tall cliffs fir; by pools the poplar-tree. 70
>
> But if thou come here oft, sweet Lycidas,
>> Lawn-pine and mountain-ash must yield to thee."

M. All this I've heard before: remember well
How Thyrsis strove in vain against defeat.
From that day forth 'twas 'Corydon' for me.

ECLOGUE VIII.

ALPHESIBŒUS'S and Damon's muse—
Charmed by whose strife the steer forgot to
 graze;
Whose notes made lynxes motionless, and bade
Rivers turn back and listen—sing we next:
Alphesibœus's and Damon's muse.

Winn'st thou the crags of great Timavus now,
Or skirtest strands where break Illyrian seas?
I know not. But oh when shall that day dawn
When I may tell thy deeds? give earth thy lays,
That match alone the pomp of Sophocles?   10
With thee began, with thee shall end, my song:
Accept what thou didst ask; and round thy brow
Twine this poor ivy with thy victor bays.

'Twas at the hour when night's cold shadow scarce
Had left the skies; when, blest by herdsmen, hangs
The dewdrop on the grass; that Damon leaned
On his smooth olive-staff, and thus began.

" Wake, morning star! Prevent warm day, and
 come!

While, duped and humbled, I—because I loved
Nisa with all a husband's love—complain ;   20
And call the gods, (though naught their cognizance
Availed,) at my last hour, a dying man.
Begin, my flute, a song of Arcady.

" There forests murmur aye, and pines discourse ;
And lovelorn swains, and Pan, who first reclaimed
From idleness the reed, hath audience there,
Begin, my flute, a song of Arcady.

" Nisa—is aught impossible in love ?—
Is given to Mopsus.   Griffins next will mate
With mares : our children see the coward deer   30
Come with the hound to drink. Go, shape the
   torch,
Mopsus! fling, bridegroom, nuts! Thou lead'st a
   wife
Home, and o'er Œta peers the evening star.
Begin, my flute, a song of Arcady.

" Oh, mated with a worthy husband ! thou
Who scorn'st mankind—abhorr'st this pipe, these
   goats
Of mine, and shaggy brows, and hanging beard :
Nor think'st that gods can see what mortals do !
Begin, my flute, a song of Arcady.

"Within our orchard-walls I saw thee first, 40
A wee child with her mother—(I was sent
To guide you)—gathering apples wet with dew.
Ten years and one I scarce had numbered then;
Could scarce on tiptoe reach the brittle boughs.
I saw, I fell, I was myself no more.
Begin, my flute, a song of Arcady.

"Now know I what love is. On hard rocks born
Tmaros, or Rhodope, or they who dwell
In utmost Africa do father him;
No child of mortal blood or lineage. 50
Begin, my flute, a song of Arcady.

"In her son's blood a mother dipped her hands
At fierce love's bidding. Hard was her heart too—
Which harder? her heart or that knavish boy's?
Knavish the boy, and hard was her heart too.
Begin, my flute, a song of Arcady.

"Now let the wolf first turn and fly the sheep:
Hard oaks bear golden apples: daffodil
Bloom on the alder: and from myrtle-stems
Ooze richest amber. Let owls vie with swans;
And be as Orpheus—Orpheus in the woods,

Arion with the dolphins—every swain,   62
(Begin, my flute, a song of Arcady)

"And earth become mid ocean. Woods, farewell!
Down from some breezy mountain height to the waves
I'll fling me. Take this last gift ere I die.
Unlearn, my flute, the songs of Arcady."

Thus Damon. How the other made reply
Sing, sisters. Scarce may all do everything.

A.   "Fetch water: wreathe yon altar with soft wool: 70
And burn rich vervain and brave frankincense;
That I may try my lord's clear sense to warp
With dark rites. Naught is lacking save the songs.
Bring, songs, bring Daphnis from the city home.

"Songs can bring down the very moon from heaven.
Circe with songs transformed Ulysses' crew.
Songs shall in sunder burst the cold grass-snake.
Bring, songs, bring Daphnis from the city home.

"Three threads about thee, of three several hues,
I twine; and thrice—(odd numbers please the
    god)—   80
Carry thy image round the altar-stones.
Bring, songs, bring Daphnis from the city home.

"Weave, Amaryllis, in three knots three hues.
Just weave and say 'I'm weaving chains of love.'
Bring, songs, bring Daphnis from the city home.

"As this clay hardens, melts this wax, at one
And the same flame: so Daphnis 'neath my love.
Strew meal, and light with pitch the crackling bay.
Daphnis burns me; for Daphnis burn these bays.
Bring, songs, bring Daphnis from the city home. 90

"Be his such longing as the heifer feels,
When, faint with seeking her lost mate through
    copse
And deepest grove, beside some water-brook
In the green grass she sinks in her despair,
Nor cares to yield possession to the night.
Be his such longing: mine no wish to heal.
Bring, songs, bring Daphnis from the city home.

"Pledges of love, these clothes the traitor once
Bequeathed me. I commit them, Earth, to thee

Here at my threshold.   He is bound by these. 100
Bring, songs, bring Daphnis from the city home.

"These deadly plants great Mœris gave to me,
In Pontus plucked: in Pontus thousands grow.
By their aid have I seen him skulk in woods
A wolf, unsepulchre the buried dead,
And charm to other fields the standing corn.
Bring, songs, bring Daphnis from the city home.

"Go, Amaryllis, ashes in thy hand:
Throw them—and look not backwards—o'er thy
    head
Into a running stream.   These next I'll try   110
On Daphnis; who regards not gods nor songs.
Bring, songs, bring Daphnis from the city home.

"See!   While I hesitate, a quivering flame
Hath clutched the wood, self-issuing from the ash.
May this mean good!   Something—for Hylas too
Barks at the gate—it must mean.   Is it true?
Or are we lovers dupes of our own dreams?
Cease, songs, cease.   Daphnis comes from the city
    home!"

ECLOGUE IX.

Lycidas. Mœris.

L.

Mœris, on foot? and on the road to town?
   M. Oh Lycidas!—we live to tell—how one—
(Who dreamed of this?)—a stranger—holds our farm,
And says, "'Tis mine: its ancient lords, begone!"
Beaten, cast down—for Chance is lord of all—
We send him—bootlessly mayhap—these kids.

L.   Yet all, I heard, from where we lose yon hills,
With gradual bend down-sloping to the brook,
And those old beeches, broken columns now,
Had your Menalcas rescued by his songs.   10

M.   Thou heardst. Fame said so. But our songs avail,
Mœris, no more 'mid warspears than, they say,
Dodona's doves may, when the eagle stoops.
A boding raven from a rifted oak
Warned me, by this means or by that to nip
This strange strife in the bud: or dead were now
Thy Mœris; dead were great Menalcas too.

L. Could such curse fall on man? Had we so near
Lost thee, Menalcas, and thy pleasantries?
Who then would sing the nymphs? Who strow with flowers   20
The ground, or train green darkness o'er the springs?
And oh! that song, which I (saying ne'er a word)
Copied one day—(while thou wert off to see
My darling, Amaryllis,)—from thy notes:
"Feed, while I journey but a few short steps,
Tityrus, my goats: and, Tityrus, when they've fed,
Lead them to drink: and cross not by the way
The he-goat's path: his horns are dangerous."

M. But that to Varus, that unfinished one!
"Varus! thy name, if Mantua still be ours—   30
(Mantua! to poor Cremona all too near,)—
Shall tuneful swans exalt unto the stars."

L. Begin, if in thee's aught. So may not yews
Of Cyrnus lure thy bees: so, clover-fed,
Thy cattle teem with milk. Me too the muse
Hath made a minstrel: I have songs; and me
The swains call 'poet.' But I heed them not.
For scarce yet sing I as the great ones sing,
But, a goose, cackle among piping swans.

M.   Indeed, I am busy turning o'er and o'er—   40
    In hopes to recollect it—in my brain
    A song, and not a mean one, Lycidas.
      " Come, Galatea! sport'st thou in the waves?
    Here spring is purpling; thick by river-banks
    Bloom the gay flowers; white poplar climbs above
    The caves, and young vines plait a roof between.
    Come! and let mad seas beat against the shore."

L.   What were those lines that once I heard thee sing,
    All uncompanioned on a summer night—
    I know the music, if I had the words.   50

M.   " Daphnis! why watch those old-world planets rise?
    Lo! onward marches sacred Cæsar's star,
    The star that made the valleys laugh with corn,
    And grapes grow ruddier upon sunny hills.
    Sow, Daphnis, pears, whereof thy sons shall eat."
    —Time carries all—our memories e'en—away.
    Well I remember how my boyish songs   57
    Would oft outlast the livelong summer day.
    And now they're all forgot. His very voice
    Hath Mœris lost: on Mœris wolves have looked.

—But oft thou'lt hear them from Menalcas yet.
L. Thy pleas but draw my passion out. And lo!
All hushed to listen is the wide sea-floor,
And laid the murmurings of the soughing winds.
And now we're half-way there. I can descry
Bianor's grave. Here, Mœris, where the swains
Are raking off the thick leaves, let us sing.
Or, if we fear lest night meanwhile bring up
The rain clouds, singing let us journey on—
(The way will seem less tedious)—journey on
Singing: and I will ease thee of thy load.
M. Cease, lad. We'll do what lies before us now:
Then sing our best, when comes the Master home.

ECLOGUE X.

GALLUS.

OH Arethuse, let this last task be mine!
   One song—a song Lycoris' self may read—
My Gallus asks: who'd grudge one song to him?
So, when thou slid'st beneath Sicilian seas,

May ne'er salt Doris mix her stream with thine:
Begin: and sing—while yon blunt muzzles search
The underwood—of Gallus torn by love.
We lack not audience: woods take up the notes.
   Where were ye, Naiad Nymphs, in grove or
      glen,
When Gallus died of unrequited love?   10
Not heights of Pindus or Parnassus, no
Aonian Aganippe kept ye then.
Him e'en the laurels wept and myrtle-groves.
Stretch'd 'neath the lone cliff, piny Mænalus
And chill Lycæum's stones all wept for him.
The sheep stood round. They think not scorn of us;
And think not scorn, O priest of song, of them.
Sheep fair Adonis fed beside the brooks.
The shepherds came. The lazy herdsmen came.
Came, from the winter acorns dripping-wet,   20
Menalcas. "Whence," all ask, "this love of
      thine?"
Apollo came: and, "Art thou mad," he saith,
"Gallus? Thy love, through bristling camps and
      snows,
Tracks now another's steps." Silvanus came,
Crowned with his woodland glories: to and fro
Rocked the great lilies and the fennel bloom.
Pan came, Arcadia's Pan: (I have seen him, red
With elder-berries and with cinnabar:)

"Is there no end?" quoth he: "Love heeds not
         this:
Tears sate not cruel Love: nor rills the leas,   30
Nor the bees clover, nor green boughs the goat."
But he rejoins sad-faced: "Yet sing this song
Upon your hills, Arcadians! none but ye
Can sing. Oh! pleasantly will rest my bones,
If pipe of yours shall one day tell my loves.
Oh! had I been as you are! kept your flocks,
Or gleaned, a vintager, your mellow grapes!
A Phyllis, an Amyntas—whom you will—
Had been my passion—what if he be dark?
Violets are dark and hyacinths are dark.—   40
And now should we be sitting side by side,
Willows around us and a vine o'erhead,
He carolling, or plucking garlands she.
—Here are cold springs, Lycoris, and soft lawns,
And woods: with thee I'd here decay and die.
Now, for grim war accoutred, all for love,
In the fray's centre I await the foe:
Thou, in a far land—out the very thought!—
Gazest (ah wilful!) upon Alpine snows
And the froz'n Rhine—without me—all alone!   50
May that frost harm not thee! that jaggèd ice
Cut ne'er thy dainty feet! I'll go, and play
My stores of music—fashioned for the lyre
Of Chalcis—on the pipe of Arcady.

My choice is made. In woods, mid wild beasts' dens,
I'll bear my love, and carve it on the trees:
That with their growth, my loves may grow and
    grow.
Banded with nymphs I'll roam o'er Mænalus,
Or hunt swift boars; and circle with my dogs,
Unrecking of the cold, Parthenia's glades.   60
Already over crag and ringing grove
I am borne in fancy: laugh as I let loose
The Cretan arrow from the Parthian bow :—

Pooh! will this heal thy madness? will that god
Learn mercy from the agonies of men?
'Tis past: again nymphs, music, fail to please.
Again I bid the very woods begone.
No deed of mine can change him: tho' I drink
Hebrus in mid December: tho' I plunge   69
In snows of Thrace, the dripping winter's snows:
Tho', when the parched bark dies on the tall elm,
'Neath Cancer's star I tend the Æthiop's sheep.
Love's lord of all. Let me too yield to Love.

        *   *   *   *

—Sung are, oh holy ones, your minstrel's songs:
Who sits here framing pipes with slender reed.
In Gallus' eyes will ye enhance their worth:
Gallus—for whom each hour my passion grows,

As swell green alders when the spring is young.
I rise. The shadows are the singer's bane:
Baneful the shadow of the juniper. 80
E'en the flocks like not shadow. Go—the star
Of morning breaks—go home, my full-fed sheep.

FROM HORACE'S ODES.

FROM HORACE'S ODES.

BOOK I.

ODE 9.

To Thaliarchus.

ONE dazzling mass of solid snow
    Soracte stands; the bent woods fret
    Beneath their load; and, sharpest-set
With frost, the streams have ceased to flow.

Pile on great faggots and break up
    The ice: let influence more benign
    Enter with four-years-treasured wine,
Fetched in the ponderous Sabine cup:

Leave to the gods all else. When they
    Have once bid rest the winds that war
    Over the passionate seas, no more
Grey ash and cypress rock and sway.

Ask not what future suns shall bring.
　　Count to-day gain, whate'er it chance
　　To be: nor, young man, scorn the dance,
Nor deem sweet Love an idle thing,

Ere time thy April youth hath changed
　　To sourness.　Park and public walk
　　Attract thee now, and whispered talk
At twilight meetings pre-arranged;

Hear now the pretty laugh that tells
　　In what dim corner lurks thy love;
And snatch a bracelet or a glove
　　From wrist or hand that scarce rebels.

ODE 11.

To Leuconöe.

SEEK not, for thou shalt not find it, what my
　　end, what thine shall be;
Ask not of Chaldæa's science what God wills,
　　Leuconöe:

Better far, what comes, to bear it. Haply many a
    wintry blast
Waits thee still; and this, it may be, Jove ordains
    to be thy last,
Which flings now the flagging sea-wave on the
    obstinate sandstone-reef.
Be thou wise: fill up the wine-cup; shortening,
    since the time is brief,
Hopes that reach into the future. While I speak,
    hath stol'n away
Jealous Time. Mistrust To-morrow, catch the
    blossom of To-day.

ODE 14.

To a Ship.

YET on fresh billows seaward wilt thou ride,
  O Ship? What dost thou? Seek a hav'n,
    and there
  Rest thee: for lo! thy side
    Is oarless all and bare,

And the swift south-west wind hath maimed thy mast,
And thy yards creak, and, every cable lost,

Yield must thy keel at last
   On tyrannous sea-waves tossed

Too rudely. Goodly canvas is not thine,
Nor gods, to hear thee when thy need is sorest:—
   True, thou—a Pontic pine,
      Child of a stately forest—

Boast'st rank and empty name: but little trust
The frightened seamen in a painted stern.
   Stay—or be mocked thou must
      By every wind in turn.

Flee—what of late sore burden was to me,
Now a sad memory and a bitter pain,—
   Those shining Cyclads flee,
      That stud the far-off main.

ODE 24.

To Virgil.

UNSHAMED, unchecked, for one so dear
   We sorrow. Lead the mournful choir,
Melpomene, to whom thy sire
Gave harp, and song-notes liquid-clear!

Sleeps He the sleep that knows no morn?
   Oh Honour, oh twin-born with Right
   Pure Faith, and Truth that loves the light,
When shall again his like be born?

Many a kind heart for Him makes moan;
   Thine, Virgil, first. But ah! in vain
   Thy love bids heaven restore again
That which it took not as a loan:

Were sweeter lute than Orpheus given
   To thee, did trees thy voice obey;
   The blood revisits not the clay
Which He, with lifted wand, hath driven

Into his dark assemblage, who
   Unlocks not fate to mortal's prayer.
   Hard lot! Yet light their griefs who BEAR
The ills, which they may not undo.

ODE 28.

To Archytas.

MEASURER of earth and ocean and the multi-
    tudinous sand,
  Scant the grains of tributary dust,
Lack whereof, Archytas, holds thee captive on
    Apulia's strand.
  Vainly in his wisdom did he trust,
Who could journey disembodied o'er the firmament,
    and stand
  At the gates of heaven; for die he must.
Perished thus the sire of Pelops, messmate of the
    gods above:
  Thus Tithonus, caught into the air:
Minos too, the man admitted to the hidden things
    of Jove.
  Pantheus' son himself is prisoner there—
In those shades—twice doomed to Orcus: tho' the
    letters on the shield
  Proved how he had lived in Ilion's day,
Nor had aught, save skin and sinew, unto grim
    death deigned to yield.

No mean scholar he, e'en thou would'st say,
In the lore of truth and nature. But the fate of
    all is sealed:
All must tread, unlighted, death's highway.
—Into grisly War's arena some are by the Furies
    flung:
'Neath the hungry sea-wave some lie dead:
Fused in undistinguished slaughter die the old man
    and the young:
Spares not Hell's fierce queen a single head.
Me too westward-bound Orion's constant mate, the
    South-west-wind,
Whelmed but lately in the Illyrian wave:
And, oh mariner, deny not—to a dead man's bones
    unkind,
And a head that must not own a grave—
One scant heap of homeless sea-sand. So whene'er
    the Eastern gale
Chides the South seas, may his fury lay
Green Etruria's woods in ruin, sparing thee: so
    many a bale
Drop to thee, whence only drop it may,
From great Jove, and Neptune watching o'er Ta-
    rentum's holy soil.
—Wilt commit, unrecking, an offence
Which shall harm thy innocent offspring? On thine
    own head may recoil

Righteous vengeance, and a recompense
That shall bow thy pride.   Abandoned, unavenged,
　　I will not be:
For such crime no offerings shall atone.
Though mayhap thy time is precious, small the boon
　　I ask of thee:
Throw three handfuls o'er me, and begone.

ODE 38.

To his Slave.

PERSIAN grandeur I abhor:
　　Linden-wreathèd crowns, avaunt:
Boy, I bid thee not explore
　　Woods which latest roses haunt:

Try on naught thy busy craft
　　Save plain myrtle; so arrayed
Thou shalt fetch, I drain, the draught
　　Fitliest 'neath the scant vine-shade.

BOOK III.

ODE 1.

I SCORN and shun the rabble's noise.
    Abstain from idle talk. A thing
    That ear hath not yet heard, I sing,
The Muses' priest, to maids and boys.

To Jove the flocks which great kings sway,
    To Jove great kings allegiance owe.
    Praise him: he laid the giants low:
All things that are, his nod obey.

This man may plant in broader lines
    His fruit-trees: that, the pride of race
    Enlists a candidate for place:
In worth, in fame, a third outshines

His mates; or, thronged with clients, claims
    Precedence. Even-handed Fate
    Hath but one law for small and great:
That ample urn holds all men's names.

He o'er whose doomed neck hangs the sword
    Unsheathed, the dainties of the South
    Shall lack their sweetness in his mouth:
No note of bird or harpsichord

Shall bring him Sleep. Yet Sleep is kind,
    Nor scorns the huts of labouring men;
    The bank where shadows play, the glen
Of Tempe dancing in the wind.

He, who but asks 'Enough,' defies
    Wild waves to rob him of his ease;
    He fears no rude shocks, when he sees
Arcturus set or Hædus rise:

When hailstones lash his vines, or fails
    His farm its promise, now of rains
    And now of stars that parch the plains
Complaining, or unkindly gales.

—In straitened seas the fish are pent;
    For dams are sunk into the deep:
    Pile upon pile the builders heap,
And he, whom earth could not content,

The Master. Yet shall Fear and Hate
    Climb where the Master climbs: nor e'er

From the armed trireme parts black Care;
He sits behind, the horseman's mate.

And if red marble shall not ease
    The heartache; nor the shell that shines
    Star-bright; nor all Falernum's vines,
All scents that charmed Achæmenes:

Why should I rear me halls of rare
    Design, on proud shafts mounting high?
    Why bid my Sabine vale goodbye
For doubled wealth and doubled care?

ODE 2.

FRIEND! with a poor man's straits to fight
    Let warfare teach thy stalwart boy:
    Let him the Parthian's front annoy
With lance in rest, a dreaded knight:

Live in the field, inure his eye
    To danger. From the foeman's wall
    May the armed tyrant's dame, with all
Her damsels, gaze on him, and sigh,

" Dare not, in war unschooled, to rouse
    Yon Lion—whom to touch is death,
    To whom red Anger ever saith,
'*Slay and slay on*'—O prince, my spouse!"

—Honoured and blest the patriot dies.
    From death the recreant may not flee:
    Death shall not spare the faltering knee
And coward back of him that flies.

Valour—unbeat, unsullied still—
    Shines with pure lustre: all too great
    To seize or drop the sword of state,
Swayed by a people's veering will.

Valour—to souls too great for death
    Heav'n op'ning—treads the untrodden way:
    And this dull world, this damp cold clay,
On wings of scorn, abandoneth.

—Let too the sealed lip honoured be.
    The babbler, who'd the secrets tell
    Of holy Ceres, shall not dwell
Where I dwell; shall not launch with me

A shallop. Heaven full many a time
    Hath with the unclean slain the just:
    And halting-footed Vengeance must
O'ertake at last the steps of crime.

ODE 3.

THE just man's single-purposed mind
    Not furious mobs that prompt to ill
    May move, nor kings' frowns shake his will
Which is as rock; not warrior winds

That keep the seas in wild unrest;
    Nor bolt by Jove's own finger hurled:
    The fragments of a shivered world
Would crash round him still self-possest.

Jove's wandering son reached, thus endowed,
    The fiery bastions of the skies;
    Thus Pollux; with them Cæsar lies
Beside his nectar, radiant-browed.

Honoured for this, by tigers drawn
    Rode Bacchus, reining necks before
    Untamed; for this War's horses bore
Quirinus up from Acheron.

To the pleased gods had Juno said
    In conclave: "Troy is in the dust;
    Troy, by a judge accursed, unjust,
And that strange woman prostrated.

"The day Laomedon ignored
    His god-pledged word, resigned to me
    And Pallas ever pure, was she,
Her people, and their traitor lord.

"Now the Greek woman's guilty guest
    Dazzles no more: Priam's perjured sons
    Find not against the mighty ones
Of Greece a shield in Hector's breast:

"And, long drawn out by private jars,
    The war sleeps. Lo! my wrath is o'er:
    And him the Trojan vestal bore
(Sprung of that hated line) to Mars,

"To Mars restore I. His be rest
    In halls of light: by him be drained
    The nectar-bowl, his place obtained
In the calm companies of the blest.

"While betwixt Rome and Ilion raves
    A length of ocean, where they will
    Rise empires for the exiles still:
While Paris's and Priam's graves

"Are trod by kine, and she-wolves breed
    Securely there, unharmed shall stand

Rome's lustrous Capitol, her hand
Curb with proud laws the trampled Mede.

" Wide-feared, to far-off climes be borne
    Her story; where the central main
    Europe and Libya parts in twain,
Where full Nile laves a land of corn:

" The buried secret of the mine,
    (Best left there) let her dare to spurn,
    Nor unto man's base uses turn
Profane hands laying on things divine.

" Earth's utmost end, where'er it be,
    Let her hosts reach; careering proud
    O'er lands where watery rain and cloud,
Or where wild suns hold revelry.

" But, to the warriors of Rome,
    Tied by this law, such fates are willed;
    That they seek never to rebuild,
Too fond, too bold, their grandsires' home.

" With darkest omens, deadliest strife,
    Shall Troy, raised up again, repeat
    Her history; I the victor-fleet
Shall lead, Jove's sister and his wife.

"Thrice let Apollo rear the wall
  Of brass; and thrice my Greeks shall hew
  The fabric down: thrice matrons rue
In chains their sons', their husbands' fall."

Ill my light lyre such notes beseem.
  Stay, Muse; nor, wayward still, rehearse
  Sayings of Gods in meagre verse
That may but mar a mighty theme.

ODE 4.

COME, Music's Queen, from yonder sphere:
  Bid thy harp speak: sing high and higher—
  Or take Apollo's lute and lyre,
And play, and cease not. Did ye hear?

Or is some sweet Delusion mine?
  I seem to hear, to stray beside
  Groves that are holy; whither glide
Fair brooks, where breezes are benign.

Me, on mount Vultur once—a lad,
  O'ercome with sleepiness and play—

(I had left Apulia miles away,
That nursed me) doves from Fayland clad

With leaflets. Marvelled all whose nest
    Is Acherontia's cliff; who fell
      The Bantine forest trees, or dwell
On rich Ferentium's lowly breast;

How I could sleep, unharmed by bear
    Or dusky serpent. There I lay,
      In myrtle hid and holy bay,
A lusty babe, the Great ones' care.

Yours, Sisters, yours, the Sabine hills
    I climb: at cool Præneste yours,
      Yours by flat Tibur, or the shores
Of Baiæ. I have loved your rills,

Your choirs: for this Philippi's slaughter,
    When fled our captains, harmed not me;
      I died not 'neath the cursed tree,
Nor sank in Palinurus' water :—

Be with me still: and, fears at rest,
    I'll launch on raving Bosphorus, stand
      Upon Assyria's sultry sand,
With Britons mate, who slay the guest,

Sit down with Spaniards, wild to sate
    Their thirst with horses' blood; or roam
    Far o'er the quivered Scythian's home
By Tanais' banks, inviolate.

—High Cæsar ye (his war-worn braves
    Safe housed at last in thorp and town)
    Asking to lay his labours down,
Make welcome in Pierian caves.

—Kind ones! Ye give sweet counsel, love
    Its givers. *We* know how he slew
    The Titans, and their hideous crew,
Hurling his thunder from above,

Who the dull earth, the windy sea,
    The cities, and the realms of woe,
    And gods above, and men below,
Rules, and none other, righteously.

In truth Jove's terrors had been great;
    So bold a front those warriors shewed
    Those brethren, on his dark abode
Striving to pile all Pelion's weight.

But Mimas and Typhoëus were
    As naught, and huge Porphyrion too,

And Rhœcus, and the arm that threw,
Undaunted, tree-trunks through the air;

With ringing shield when Pallas met
    Their rush. Hot Vulcan too stood there,
    And Juno sage, and he, who ne'er
Eased from the bow his shoulder yet;

Who bathes in pure Castalian dew
    His locks; in Lycian bowers adored,
    And his own woods,—Apollo, lord
Of Delos and of Patara too.

—Brute force its own bulk foils. But force
    By reason led, the gods make great
    And greater; while the strong they hate,
Whose brain revolves each evil course.

This Gyas, hundred-armed, could tell;
    And that Orion, who with wild
    Violence assailed the Undefiled,
And by Diana's arrows fell.

—Earth, grieved, her monster brood entombed:
    Mourns them, by Jove's bolts hurled to hell.
    Still living fires 'neath Ætna dwell,
Yet Ætna still is unconsumed:

O'er wanton Tityus' heart the bird,
    That miscreant's gaoler, still doth hover;
    And still Pirithöus, lawless lover,
Do thrice a hundred fetters gird.

ODE 5.

JOVE we call King, whose bolts rive heaven:
    Then a god's *presence* shall be felt
    In Cæsar, with whose power the Celt
And Parthian stout in vain have striven.

Could Crassus' men wed alien wives,
    And greet, as sons-in-law, the foe?
    In the foes' land (oh Romans, oh
Lost honour!) end, in shame, their lives,

'Neath the Mede's sway? They, Marsians and
    Apulians—shields and rank and name
    Forgot, and that undying flame—
And Jove still reign, and Rome still stand?

This thing wise Regulus could presage:
    He brooked not base conditions; he

Set not a precedent to be
The ruin of a coming age:

" No," cried he, " let the captives die,
    Spare not. I saw Rome's ensigns hung
    In Punic shrines; with sabres, flung
Down by Rome's sons ere blood shed. I

" Saw our free citizens with hands
    Fast pinioned; and, through portals now
    Flung wide, our soldiers troop to plough,
As once they trooped to waste, the lands.

" ' Bought by our gold, our men will fight
    But keener.' What? To shame would you
    Add loss? As wool, its natural hue
Once gone, may not be *painted* white;

" True Valour, from her seat once thrust,
    Is not replaced by meaner wares.
    Do stags, delivered from the snares,
Fight? Then shall *he* fight, who did trust

" His life to foes who spoke a lie:
    And *his* sword shatter Carthage yet,
    Around whose arms the cords have met,
A sluggard soul, that feared to die!

"Life, howe'er bought, he treasured : he
    Deemed war a thing of trade. Ah fie!—
    Great art thou, Carthage—towerest high
O'er shamed and ruined Italy!"

As one uncitizen'd—men said—
    He put his wife's pure kiss away.
    His little children; and did lay
Stern in the dust his manly head:

Till those unequalled words had lent
    Strength to the faltering sires of Rome;
    Then from his sorrow-stricken home
Went forth to glorious banishment.

Yet knew he, what wild tortures lay
    Before him: knowing, put aside
    His kin, his countrymen—who tried
To bar his path, and bade him stay:

He might be hastening on his way,—
    A lawyer freed from business—down
    To green Venafrum, or a town
Of Sparta, for a holiday.

ODE 6.

THOU 'lt rue thy fathers' sins, not thine,
    Till built the temples be, replaced
    The statues, foul and smoke-defaced,—
Roman,—and reared each tottering shrine.

Thou rul'st but under heaven's hand.
    Thence all beginnings come, all ends.
    Neglected, mark what woes it sends
On this our miserable land.

Twice Pacorus and Monæses foiled
    Our luckless onset: huge their glee,
    When to their necklaces they see
Hanging the wealth of Rome despoiled.

Dacian and Æthiop nigh laid low
    Our state, with civil feuds o'errun;
    One with his fleet dismayed her, one
Smote her with arrows from his bow.

A guilty age polluted first
    Our birds, hearths, families: from that source

Derived, the foul stream, gathering force,
O'er the broad land, a torrent, burst.

Pleased, now, the maiden learns to move
    To soft Greek airs : already knows—
    Fresh from the nursery—how to pose
Her graceful limbs; and dreams of love :

Next, while her lord drinks deep, invites
    Her gallants in : nor singles one,
    Into whose guilty arms to run,
Stealthy and swift, when dim the lights :

No ! in her lord's sight up springs she :
    Alike at some small tradesman's beck,
    As his who walks a Spanish deck
And barters wealth for infamy.

—Were those lads of such parents bred
    Who dyed the seas with Punic blood ?
    Pyrrhus, Antiochus withstood,
And Hannibal, the nation's dread ?

Rude soldiers' sons, a rugged kind,
    They brake the soil with Sabine spade :
    Or shouldered stakes their axe had made
To a right rigorous mother's mind,

What time the shadows of the rocks
    Change, as the sun's departing car
    Sends on the hours that sweetest are,
And men unyoke the wearied ox.

Time mars not—what? A spoiler he.
    Our sires were not so brave a breed
    As *their* sires: we, a worse, succeed;
To raise up sons more base than we.

ODE 13.

To the Fountain of Bandusia.

BANDUSIA, stainless mirror of the sky!
    Thine is the flower-crown'd bowl, for thee shall die,
      When dawns yon sun, the kid;
      Whose horns, half-seen, half-hid,

Challenge to dalliance or to strife—in vain!
Soon must the firstling of the wild herd be slain,
      And those cold springs of thine
      With blood incarnadine.

Fierce glows the Dogstar, but his fiery beam
Toucheth not thee : still grateful thy cool stream
    To labour-wearied ox,
    Or wanderer from the flocks:

And hence forth thou shalt be a royal fountain:
My harp shall tell how from yon cavernous mountain,
    Where the brown oak grows tallest,
    All babblingly thou fallest.

ODE 18.

To a Faun.

WOOER of young Nymphs who fly thee,
    Lightly o'er my sunlit lawn,
Trip, and go, nor injured by thee
    Be my weanling herds, O Faun:

If the kid his doomed head bows, and
    Brims with wine the loving cup,
When the year is full; and thousand
    Scents from altars hoar go up.

Each flock in the rich grass gambols
    When the month comes which is thine;
And the happy village rambles
    Fieldward with the idle kine:

Lambs play on, the wolf their neighbour:
    Wild woods deck thee with their spoil;
And with glee the sons of labour
    Stamp upon their foe the soil.

BOOK IV.

ODE 13.

To Lyce.

LYCE, the gods have listened to my prayer:
　The gods have listened, Lyce. Thou art gray
　　And still would'st thou seem fair;
　　　Still unshamed drink, and play,

And, wine-flushed, woo slow-answering Love with weak
Shrill pipings. With young Chia He doth dwell,
　　Queen of the harp: her cheek
　　　Is his sweet citadel:—

He marked the withered oak, and on he flew
Intolerant; shrank from Lyce grim and wrinkled,
　　Whose teeth are ghastly-blue,
　　　Whose temples snow-besprinkled:—

Not purple, not the brightest gem that glows,
Brings back to her the years which, fleeting fast,
　　Time hath once shut in those
　　　Dark annals of the Past.

Oh, where is all thy loveliness? soft hue
And motions soft? Oh, what of Her doth rest,
    Her, who breathed love, who drew
        My heart out of my breast?

Fair, and far-famed, and subtly sweet, thy face
Ranked next to Cinara's. But to Cinara fate
    Gave but a few years' grace;
        And lets live, all too late,

Lyce, the rival of the beldam crow:
That fiery youth may see with scornful brow
    The torch that long ago
        Beamed bright, a cinder now.

EPODE 2.

"HAPPY—who far from turmoil, like the men
    That lived in days gone by,
With his own oxen ploughs his native glen,
    Nor dreams of usury!
Him the fierce clarion summons not to war;
    He dreads not angry seas:
The courts—the stately citizens' proud door—

  He gets him far from these.
His maiden-vines it is his gentle craft
  With poplars tall to wed:
Or the rank outgrowth lopping off, ingraft
  Fair branches in its stead;
To watch his kine, that wander, lowing, far
  Into the valley deep:
Store the prest honey in the taintless jar,
  Or shear his tender sheep.

And soon as Autumn, with fair fruitage tricked,
  Peeps o'er the fallows bare;
Then with what glee his purpling grape is picked,
  And newly-grafted pear,
For you, Priapus and Silvanus—strict
  Guard of his land—to share.

—Now 'neath an ancient oak, entangled now
  In green grass, will he lie;
Where streams go by bank-hidden; from the bough
  Is heard the wood-birds' cry;
And brawls the clear brook, as if seeking how
  To sing him lullaby.

—But when the wintry skies Jove's thunder rives,
  And down the snow-storms pour;
Towards the set pit-fall, doubling oft, he drives
  The hound-encompassed boar:
Or with smooth rods his web of nets prepares,
  The fat thrush to surprise;

Or nooses stranger cranes, or frightened hares—
    Either a glorious prize!
Who, with such pleasures round him, for the cares
    That fret a lover sighs?

" Does a pure wife his household cares divide,
    Watch his sweet little ones;—
(The Sabine's thus and swift Apulian's bride
    Toiled 'neath Apulia's suns;)—
The sacred hearth with seasoned faggots heap,
    When her tired lord draws nigh;
And hurdling, nothing loth, her folded sheep,
    Drain their great udders dry:
Then the last vintage draw from the sweet cask
    To grace the home-made feast?—
For Lucrine purple-fish I shall not ask,
    Nor turbots from the East:
Not char, which—thundering first o'er other seas—
    Storms carried to our shore,
Not woodcocks from Ionia would please,
    Or hens from Guinea, more
My taste; than oil that, in the rich boughs hid,
    Her hands did thence obtain;
And meadow-dock, and mallow that can rid
    Our suffering frames from pain,
With lamb that bled for Terminus; and kid
    By wolves so nearly slain!

" So banqueting, how sweet to notice how
    The fed ewes homeward fare:
How oxen, half asleep, the inverted plough
    On drooping shoulders bear ;
And slaves—sure signs of wealth—ranged idle now,
    Swarm round the glad hearth's glare ! "

So did the money-lender Appius speak,
    Resolved to be a swain,
And got his money in. Within a week
    Would put it out again.

THE DEAD OX.

From Virgil, Georg. III.

LO! smoking in the stubborn plough, the ox
Falls, from his lip foam gushing crimson-stained,
And sobs his life out. Sad of face the ploughman
Moves, disentangling from his comrade's corpse
The lone surviver: and its work half-done,
Abandoned in the furrow stands the plough.
Not shadiest forest-depths, not softest lawns,
May move him now: not river amber-pure,
That tumbles o'er the cragstones to the plain.
Powerless the broad sides, glazed the rayless eye,
And low and lower sinks the ponderous neck.
What thank hath he for all the toil he toiled,
The heavy-clodded land in man's behoof
Upturning? Yet the grape of Italy,
The stored-up feast hath wrought no harm to him:
Green leaf and taintless grass are all their fare;
The clear rill or the travel-freshened stream
Their cup: nor one care mars their honest sleep.

SPEECH OF AJAX.

Soph. Aj. 645.

ALL strangest things the multitudinous years
Bring forth, and shadow from us all we know.
Falter alike great oath and steeled resolve;
And none shall say of aught, "This may not be."
Lo! I myself, but yesterday so strong,
As new-dipt steel am weak and all unsexed
By yonder woman: yea I mourn for them,
Widow and orphan, left amid their foes.
But I will journey seaward—where the shore
Lies meadow-fringed—so haply wash away
My sin, and flee that wrath that weighs me down.
And, lighting somewhere on an untrodden way,
I will bury this my lance, this hateful thing,
Deep in some earth-hole where no eye shall see—
Night and Hell keep it in the underworld!
For never to this day, since first I grasped
The gift that Hector gave, my bitterest foe,
Have I reaped aught of honour from the Greeks.
So true that byword in the mouths of men,
"A foeman's gifts are no gifts, but a curse."

Wherefore henceforward shall I know that God
Is great; and strive to honour Atreus' sons.

Princes they are, and should be obeyed. How else?
Do not all terrible and most puissant things
Yet bow to loftier majesties? The Winter,
Who walks forth scattering snows, gives place anon
To fruitage-laden Summer; and the orb
Of weary Night doth in her turn stand by,
And let shine out, with his white steeds, the Day.
Stern tempest-blasts at last sing lullaby
To groaning seas: even the archtyrant, Sleep,
Doth loose his slaves, not hold them chained for ever.
And shall not mankind too learn discipline?
I know, of late experience taught, that him
Who is my foe I must but hate as one
Whom I may yet call Friend: and him who loves me
Will I but serve and cherish as a man
Whose love is not abiding. Few be they
Who, reaching Friendship's port, have there found
    rest.

    But, for these things, they shall be well. Go thou,
Lady, within, and there pray that the Gods
May fill unto the full my heart's desire.
And ye, my mates, do unto me with her
Like honour: bid young Teucer, if he come,
To care for me, but to be *your* friend still.
For where my way leads, thither I shall go;
Do ye my bidding; haply ye may hear,
Though now is my dark hour, that I have peace.

FROM LUCRETIUS. Book II.

SWEET, when the great sea's water is stirred to
    his depths by the storm winds,
Standing ashore to descry one afar-off mightily
    struggling:
Not that a neighbour's sorrow to you yields dulcet
    enjoyment;
But that the sight hath a sweetness, of ills ourselves
    are exempt from.
Sweet 'tis too to behold, on a broad plain mustering,
    war-hosts
Arm them for some great battle, one's self unscathed
    by the danger!—
Yet still happier this:—To possess, impregnably
    guarded,
Those calm heights of the sages, which have for an
    origin Wisdom;
Thence to survey our fellows, observe them this
    way and that way
Wander amidst Life's paths, poor stragglers seeking
    a highway:
Watch mind battle with mind, and escutcheon rival
    escutcheon;

Gaze on that untold strife, which is waged 'neath
    the sun and the starlight,
Up as they toil on the surface whereon rest Riches
    and Empire.
  O race born unto trouble! O minds all lacking
    of eyesight!
'Neath what a vital darkness, amidst how terrible
    dangers,
Move ye thro' this thing, Life, this fragment! Fools,
    that ye hear not
Nature clamour aloud for the one thing only; that,
    all pain
Parted and past from the Body, the Mind too bask
    in a blissful
Dream, all fear of the future and all anxiety over!
  Now, as regards Man's Body, a few things only
    are needful,
(Few, tho' we sum up all,) to remove all misery from
    him;
Aye, and to strew in his path such a lib'ral carpet
    of pleasures,
That scarce Nature herself would at times ask
    happiness ampler.
Statues of youth and of beauty may not gleam golden
    around him,
(Each in his right hand bearing a great lamp
    lustrously burning,

Whence to the midnight revel a light may be furnishèd always);
Silver may not shine softly, nor gold blaze bright, in his mansion,
Nor to the noise of the tabret his halls gold-cornicèd echo:—
Yet still he, with his fellow, reposed on the velvety greensward,
Near to a rippling stream, by a tall tree canopied over,
Shall, though they lack great riches, enjoy all bodily pleasure.
Chiefliest then, when above them a fair sky smiles, and the young year
Flings with a bounteous hand over each green meadow the wild-flowers:—
Not more quickly depart from his bosom fiery fevers,
Who beneath crimson hangings and pictures cunningly broidered
Tosses about, than from him who must lie in beggarly raiment.

 Therefore, since to the Body avail not Riches, avails not
Heraldry's utmost boast, nor the pomp and the pride of an empire;

Next shall you own, that the Mind needs likewise
    nothing of these things.
Unless—when, peradventure, your armies over the
    champaign
Spread with a stir and a ferment, and bid War's
    image awaken,
Or when with stir and with ferment a fleet sails
    forth upon Ocean—
Cowed before these brave sights, pale Superstition
    abandon
Straightway your mind as you gaze, Death seem
    no longer alarming,
Trouble vacate your bosom, and Peace hold holiday
    in you.
    But, if (again) all this be a vain impossible fiction ;
If of a truth men's fears, and the cares which hourly
    beset them,
Heed not the jav'lin's fury, regard not clashing of
    broadswords ;
But all-boldly amongst crowned heads and the
    rulers of empires
Stalk, not shrinking abashed from the dazzling
    glare of the red gold,
Not from the pomp of the monarch, who walks forth
    purple-apparelled :
These things shew that at times we are bankrupt,
    surely, of Reason ;

Think too that all Man's life through a great Dark
laboureth onward.
For, as a young boy trembles, and in that mystery,
Darkness,
Sees all terrible things: so do we too, ev'n in the
daylight,
Ofttimes shudder at that, which is not more really
alarming
Than boys' fears, when they waken, and say some
danger is o'er them.
  So this panic of mind, these clouds which gather
around us,
Fly not the bright sunbeam, nor the ivory shafts
of the Day-star:
Nature, rightly revealed, and the Reason only,
dispel them.

  Now, how moving about do the prime material
atoms
Shape forth this thing and that thing; and, once
shaped, how they resolve them;
What power says unto each, This must be; how
an inherent
Elasticity drives them about Space vagrantly
onward;
I shall unfold: thou simply give all thyself to my
teaching.

Matter mingled and massed into indissoluble union
Does not exist. For we see how wastes each separate substance;
So flow piecemeal away, with the length'ning centuries, all things,
Till from our eye by degress that old self passes, and is not.
Still Universal Nature abides unchanged as aforetime.
Whereof this is the cause. When the atoms part from a substance,
That suffers loss; but another is elsewhere gaining an increase:
So that, as one thing wanes, still a second bursts into blossom,
Soon, in its turn, to be left. Thus draws this Universe always
Gain out of loss; thus live we mortals one on another.
Bourgeons one generation, and one fades. Let but a few years
Pass, and a race has arisen which was not: as in a racecourse,
One hands on to another the burning torch of Existence.

* * * * *

SONNET.

To the Island of Sirmio.

From Catullus.

G EM of all isthmuses and isles that lie,
    Fresh or salt water's children, in clear lake
Or ampler ocean: with what joy do I
    Approach thee, Sirmio! Oh! am I awake,
Or dream that once again mine eye beholds
Thee, and has looked its last on Thracian wolds?
    Sweetest of sweets to me that pastime seems,
When the mind drops her burden: when—the pain
Of travel past—our own cot we regain,
    And nestle on the pillow of our dreams!
'Tis this one thought that cheers us as we roam.
    Hail, O fair Sirmio! Joy, thy lord is here!
    Joy too, ye waters of the Golden Mere!
And ring out, all ye laughter-peals of home!

TRANSLATIONS INTO LATIN.

LYCIDAS.

YET once more, O ye laurels! and once more
   Ye myrtles brown, with ivy never sere,
I come to pluck your berries harsh and crude,
And with forced fingers rude
Shatter your leaves before the mellowing year.
Bitter constraint, and sad occasion dear,
Compels me to disturb your season due;
For Lycidas is dead, dear ere his prime,
Young Lycidas, and hath not left his peer:
Who would not sing for Lycidas? He knew
Himself to sing, and build the lofty rhyme.
He must not float upon his watery bier
Unwept, and welter to the parching wind,
Without the meed of some melodious tear.
    Begin then, sisters, of the sacred well,
That from beneath the seat of Jove doth spring;
Begin, and somewhat loudly sweep the string.
Hence with denial vain, and coy excuse,
So may some gentle muse
With lucky words favour my destined urn,
And, as he passes, turn

LYCIDAS.

EN! iterum laurus, iterum salvete myricæ
  Pallentes, nullique hederæ quæ ceditis ævo.
Has venio baccas, quanquam sapor asper acerbis,
Decerptum, quassumque manu folia ista proterva,
Maturescentem prævortens improbus annum.
Causa gravis, pia causa, subest, et amara deûm lex;
Nec jam sponte mea vobis rata tempora turbo.
Nam periit Lycidas, periit superante juventa
Imberbis Lycidas, nec par manet illius alter.
Quis cantare super Lycida neget? Ipse quoque artem
Nôrat Apollineam, versumque imponere versu.
Non nullo vitreum fas innatet ille feretrum
Flente, voluteturque arentes corpus ad auras,
Indotatum adeo et lacrymæ vocalis egenum.
  Quare agite, o sacri fontis queis cura, sorores,
Cui sub inaccessi sella Jovis exit origo:
Incipite, et sonitu graviore impellite chordas.
Lingua procul male prompta loqui, suasorque mo-
    rarum
Sit pudor: alloquiis ut mollior una secundis
Pieridum faveat, cui mox ego destiner, urnæ:
Et gressus prætergrediens convertat, et "Esto",

And bid fair peace be to my sable shroud:
For we were nursed upon the self-same hill,
Fed the same flock by fountain, shade, and rill.
    Together both, ere the high lawns appeared
Under the opening eyelids of the morn,
We drove afield, and both together heard
What time the gray fly winds her sultry horn,
Battening our flocks with the fresh dews of night,
Oft till the star that rose, at evening, bright,
Toward Heaven's descent had sloped his westering
        wheel.
Meanwhile the rural ditties were not mute,
Tempered to the oaten flute;
Rough satyrs danced, and fauns with cloven heel
From the glad sound would not be absent long,
And old Damœtas loved to hear our song.
    But oh, the heavy change, now thou art gone,
Now thou art gone, and never must return!
Thee, shepherd, thee the woods, and desert caves
With wild thyme and the gadding vine o'ergrown,
And all their echoes mourn.
The willows, and the hazel-copses green,
Shall now no more be seen,
Fanning their joyous leaves to thy soft lays.
As killing as the canker to the rose,
Or taint-worm to the weanling herds that graze,
Or frost to flowers, that their gay wardrobe wear,

Dicat, " amœna quies atra tibi veste latenti " :
Uno namque jugo duo nutribamur; eosdem
Pavit uterque greges ad fontem et rivulum et umbram.

Tempore nos illo, nemorum convexa priusquam,
Aurora reserante oculos, cœpere videri,
Urgebamus equos ad pascua : novimus horam
Aridus audiri solitus qua clangor asili;
Rore recente greges passi pinguescere noctis
Sæpius, albuerat donec quod vespere sidus
Hesperios axes prono inclinasset Olympo.
At pastorales non cessavere camœnæ,
Fistula disparibus quas temperat apta cicutis :
Saltabant Satyri informes, nec murmure læto
Capripedes potuere diu se avertere Fauni;
Damœtasque modos nostros longævus amabat.

Jamque, relicta tibi, quantum mutata videntur
Rura—relicta tibi, cui non spes ulla regressûs !
Te sylvæ, teque antra, puer, deserta ferarum,
Incultis obducta thymis ac vite sequaci,
Decessisse gemunt; gemitusque reverberat Echo.
Non salices, non glauca ergo coryleta videbo
Molles ad numeros lætum motare cacumen.
Quale rosis scabies ; quam formidabile vermis
Depulso jam lacte gregi, dum tondet agellos ;
Sive quod, indutis verna jam veste, pruinæ
Floribus, albet ubi primum paliurus in agris :

When first the white-thorn blows;
Such, Lycidas, thy loss to shepherds' ear.
    Where were ye, nymphs, when the remorseless deep
Closed o'er the head of your loved Lycidas?
For neither were ye playing on the steep,
Where your old bards, the famous Druids, lie;
Nor on the shaggy top of Mona high,
Nor yet where Deva spreads her wizard stream:
Ay me! I fondly dream!
Had ye been there, for what could that have done?
What could the muse herself that Orpheus bore,
The muse herself for her enchanting son,
Whom universal nature did lament,
When by the rout that made the hideous roar,
His gory visage down the stream was sent,
Down the swift Hebrus to the Lesbian shore?
    Alas! what boots it with incessant care
To tend the homely slighted shepherd's trade,
And strictly meditate the thankless muse?
Were it not better done as others use,
To sport with Amaryllis in the shade,
Or with the tangles of Neæra's hair?
Fame is the spur that the clear spirit doth raise
(That last infirmity of noble mind)
To scorn delights, and live laborious days,
But the fair guerdon when we hope to find,
And think to burst out into sudden blaze,

Tale fuit nostris, Lycidam periisse, bubulcis.
 Qua, Nymphæ, latuistis, ubi crudele profundum
Delicias Lycidam vestras sub vortice torsit?
Nam neque vos scopulis tum ludebatis in illis [1]
Quos veteres, Druidæ, vates, illustria servant
Nomina; nec celsæ setoso in culmine Monæ,
Nec, quos Deva locos magicis amplectitur undis.
Væ mihi! delusos exercent somnia sensus:
Venissetis enim; numquid venisse juvaret?
Numquid Pieris ipsa parens interfuit Orphei,
Pieris ipsa suæ sobolis, qui carmine rexit
Corda virum, quem terra olim, quam magna, dolebat,
Tempore quo, dirum auditu strepitante caterva,
Ora secundo amni missa, ac fœdata cruore,
Lesbia præcipitans ad litora detulit Hebrus?
 Eheu quid prodest noctes instare diesque
Pastorum curas spretas humilesque tuendo,
Nilque relaturam meditari rite Camœnam?
Nonne fuit satius lusus agitare sub umbra,
(Ut mos est aliis,) Amaryllida sive Neæram
Sectanti, ac tortis digitum impediisse capillis?
Scilicet ingenuum cor Fama, novissimus error

[1] The following alternative rendering was found amongst the author's papers:—

Quæ mora vos tenuit, Nymphæ, quum immitibus æquor
Delicias Lycidam vestras submergeret undis?
Nam neque tunc scopulis colludebatis in illis

Comes the blind fury with the abhorred shears,
And slits the thin-spun life. "But not the praise."
Phœbus replied, and touched my trembling ears;
" Fame is no plant that grows on mortal soil,
Nor in the glistering foil
Set off to the world, nor in broad rumour lies,
But lives and spreads aloft by those pure eyes,
And perfect witness of all-judging Jove;
As he pronounces lastly on each deed,
Of so much fame in Heaven expect thy meed."

  O fountain Arethuse, and thou honoured flood,
Smooth-sliding Mincius, crowned with vocal reeds,
That strain I heard was of a higher mood:
But now my oat proceeds,
And listens to the herald of the sea
That came in Neptune's plea;
He asked the waves, and asked the felon winds,
What hard mishap had doomed this gentle swain?
And questioned every gust of rugged wings,
That blows from off each beaked promontory:
They knew not of his story,
And sage Hippotades their answer brings,
That not a blast was from his dungeon strayed,
The air was calm, and on the level brine
Sleek Panope with all her sisters played.
It was that fatal and perfidious bark
Built in the eclipse, and rigged with curses dark,

Illa animi majoris, uti calcaribus urget
Spernere delicias ac dedi rebus agendis.
Quanquam—exoptatam jam spes attingere dotem;
Jam nec opinata remur splendescere flamma:—
Cæca sed invisa cum forfice venit Erinnys,
Quæ resecet tenui hærentem subtemine vitam.
" At Famam non illa," refert, tangitque trementes
Phœbus Apollo aures. "Fama haud, vulgaris ad instar
Floris, amat terrestre solum, fictosque nitores
Queis inhiat populus, nec cum Rumore patescit.
Vivere dant illi, dant increbrescere late
Puri oculi ac vox summa Jovis, cui sola Potestas.
Fecerit ille semel de facto quoque virorum
Arbitrium: tantum famæ manet æthera nactis."

 Fons Arethusa! sacro placidus qui laberis alveo,
Frontem vocali prætextus arundine, Minci!
Sensi equidem gravius carmen. Nunc cetera pastor
Exsequor. Adstat enim missus pro rege marino,
Seque rogâsse refert fluctus, ventosque rapaces,
Quæ sors dura nimis tenerum rapuisset agrestem.
Compellasse refert alarum quicquid ab omni
Spirat, acerba sonans, scopulo, qui cuspidis instar
Prominet in pelagus; fama haud pervenerat illuc.
Hæc ultro pater Hippotades responsa ferebat:
" Nulli sunt nostro palati carcere venti.
 Straverat æquor aquas, et sub Jove compta sereno

That sunk so low that sacred head of thine.
   Next Camus, reverend sire, went footing slow,
His mantle hairy, and his bonnet sedge,
Inwrought with figures dim, and on the edge,
Like to that sanguine flower inscribed with woe.
" Ah! who hath reft," quoth he, " my dearest
        pledge ? "
Last came, and last did go,
The pilot of the Galilean lake,
Two massy keys he bore, of metals twain
(The golden opes, the iron shuts amain).
He shook his mitred locks, and stern bespake:
"How well could I have spared for thee, young swain,
Enow of such as for their bellies' sake
Creep, and intrude, and climb into the fold!
Of other care they little reckoning make,
Than how to scramble at the shearer's feast,
And shove away the worthy bidden guest;
Blind mouths! that scarce themselves know how to
        hold
A sheep-hook, or have learned aught else the least
That to the faithful herdsman's art belongs!
What recks it then? What need they? They are
        sped;
And when they list, their lean and flashy songs
Grate on their scrannel pipes of wretched straw;
The hungry sheep look up, and are not fed,

Lusum exercebat Panope nymphæque sorores.
Quam Furiæ struxere per interlunia, leto
Fœtam ac fraude ratem,—malos velarat Erinnys,—
Credas in mala tanta caput mersisse sacratum."

   Proximus huic tardum senior se Camus agebat;
Cui setosa chlamys, cui pileus ulva: figuris
Idem intertextus dubiis erat, utque cruentos
Quos perhibent flores, inscriptus margine luctum.
"Nam quis," ait, "prædulce meum me pignus
     ademit?"

   Post hos, qui Galilæa regit per stagna carinas,
Post hos venit iturus: habet manus utraque clavim,
(Queis aperit clauditque) auro ferrove gravatam.
Mitra tegit crines; quassis quibus, acriter infit:
" Scilicet optassem pro te dare corpora leto
Sat multa, o juvenis: quod serpunt ventribus acti,
Vi quot iter faciunt spretis in ovilia muris.
Hic labor, hoc opus est, pecus ut tondente magistro
Præripiant epulas, trudatur dignior hospes.
Capti oculis, non ore! pedum tractare nec ipsi
Norunt; quotve bonis sunt upilionibus artes.
Sed quid enim refert, quove est opus, omnia
     nactis?
Fert ubi mens, tenue ac deductum carmen avenam
Radit stridentem stipulis. Pastore negato
Suspicit ægra pecus: vento gravis ac lue tracta
Tabescit; mox fœda capit contagia vulgus.

But swollen with wind, and the rank mist they draw,
Rot inwardly, and foul contagion spread:
Besides what the grim wolf with privy paw
Daily devours apace, and nothing said.
But that two-handed engine at the door
Stands ready to smite once, and smite no more."

Return, Alpheus, the dread voice is past,
That shrunk thy streams; return Sicilian muse,
And call the vales, and bid them hither cast
Their bells and flowerets of a thousand hues.
Ye valleys low, where the mild whispers use
Of shades, and wanton winds, and gushing brooks,
On whose fresh lap the swart star sparely looks,
Throw hither all your quaint enamelled eyes,
That on the green turf suck the honeyed showers,
And purple all the ground with vernal flowers.
Bring the rathe primrose that forsaken dies,
The tufted crow-toe, and pale jessamine,
The white pink, and the pansy freaked with jet,
The glowing violet,
The musk-rose, and the well-attired woodbine,
With cowslips wan that hang the pensive head,
And every flower that sad embroidery wears:
Bid amaranthus all his beauty shed,
And daffodillies fill their cups with tears,
To strow the laureate hearse where Lycid lies.
For so to interpose a little ease,

Quid dicam, stabulis ut clandestinus oberrans
Expleat ingluviem tristis lupus, indice nullo ?
Illa tamen bimanus custodit machina portam,
Stricta, paratque malis plagam non amplius unam."

  En, Alphee, redi ! Quibus ima cohorruit unda
Voces præteriere : redux quoque Sicelis omnes
Musa voca valles ; huc pendentes hyacinthos
Fac jaciant, teneros huc flores mille colorum.
O nemorum depressa, sonant ubi crebra susurri
Umbrarum, et salientis aquæ, Zephyrique protervi ;
Queisque virens gremium penetrare Canicula parcit :
Huc oculos, totidem mirandas vertite gemmas,
Mellitos imbres queis per viridantia rura
Mos haurire, novo quo tellus vere rubescat.
Huc ranunculus, ipse arbos, pallorque ligustri,
Quæque relicta perit, vixdum matura feratur
Primula : quique ebeno distinctus, cætera flavet
Flos, et qui specie nomen detrectat eburna.
Ardenti violæ rosa proxima fundat odores ;
Serpyllumque placens, et acerbo flexile vultu
Verbascum, ac tristem si quid sibi legit amictum.
Quicquid habes pulcri fundas, amarante : coronent
Narcissi lacrymis calices, sternantque feretrum
Tectus ubi lauro Lycidas jacet : adsit ut oti
Saltem aliquid, ficta ludantur imagine mentes.
Me miserum ! Tua nam litus, pelagusque sonorum
Ossa ferunt, queiscunque procul jacteris in oris ;

Let our frail thoughts dally with false surmise.
Ay me! whilst thee the shores and sounding seas
Wash far away, where'er thy bones are hurled,
Whether beyond the stormy Hebrides,
Where thou, perhaps, under the whelming tide
Visit'st the bottom of the monstrous world;
Or whether thou to our moist vows denied,
Sleep'st by the fable of Bellerus old,
Where the great vision of the guarded mount
Looks toward Namancos and Bayona's hold;
Look homeward, angel now, and melt with ruth:
And, O ye dolphins, waft the hapless youth.

 Weep no more, woeful shepherds, weep no more,
For Lycidas your sorrow is not dead,
Sunk though he be beneath the watery floor;
So sinks the day-star in the ocean bed,
And yet anon repairs his drooping head,
And tricks his beams, and with new-spangled ore
Flames in the forehead of the morning sky:
So Lycidas sunk low, but mounted high,
Through the dear might of him that walked the
   waves,
Where other groves and other streams along,
With nectar pure his oozy locks he laves,
And hears the unexpressive nuptial song,
In the blest kingdoms meek of joy and love.
There entertain him all the saints above,

Sive procellosas ultra Symplegadas ingens
Jam subter mare visis, alit quæ monstra profundum;
Sive (negarit enim precibus te Jupiter udis)
Cum sene Bellero, veterum qui fabula, dormis,
Qua custoditi montis prægrandis imago
Namancum atque arces longe prospectat Iberas.
Verte retro te, verte deum, mollire precando:
Et vos infaustum juvenem delphines agatis.

   Ponite jam lacrymas, sat enim flevistis, agrestes.
Non periit Lycidas, vestri mœroris origo,
Marmorei quanquam fluctus hausere cadentem.
Sic et in æquoreum se condere sæpe cubile
Luciferum videas; nec longum tempus, et effert
Demissum caput, igne novo vestitus; et aurum
Ceu rutilans, in fronte poli splendescit Eoi.
Sic obiit Lycidas, sic assurexit in altum;
Illo, quem peditem mare sustulit, usus amico.
Nunc campos alios, alia errans stagna secundum
Rorantesque lavans integro nectare crines,
Audit inauditos nobis cantari Hymenæos,
Fortunatorum sedes ubi mitis amorem
Lætitiamque affert.   Hic illum, quotquot Olympum
Prædulces habitant turbæ, venerabilis ordo,
Circumstant: aliæque canunt, interque canendum
Majestate sua veniunt abeuntque catervæ,
Illius ex oculis lacrymas arcere paratæ.
Ergo non Lycidam jam lamentantur agrestes.

In solemn troops, and sweet societies,
That sing, and singing in their glory move,
And wipe the tears for ever from his eyes.
Now, Lycidas, the shepherds weep no more;
Henceforth thou art the genius of the shore,
In thy large recompense, and shalt be good
To all that wander in that perilous flood.

    Thus sang the uncouth swain to the oaks and rills,
While the still morn went out with sandals gray,
He touched the tender stops of various quills,
With eager thought warbling his Doric lay:
And now the sun had stretched out all the hills,
And now was dropped into the western bay;
At last he rose, and twitched his mantle blue,
To-morrow to fresh woods, and pastures new.

Divus eris ripæ, puer, hoc ex tempore nobis,
Grande, nec immerito, veniens in munus; opemque
Poscent usque tuam, dubiis quot in æstubus errant.
 Hæc incultus aquis puer ilicibusque canebat;
Processit dum mane silens talaribus albis.
Multa manu teneris discrimina tentat avenis,
Dorica non studio modulatus carmina segni:
Et jam sol abiens colles extenderat omnes,
Jamque sub Hesperium se præcipitaverat alveum.
Surrexit tandem, glaucumque retraxit amictum;
Cras lucos, reor, ille novos, nova pascua quæret.

BOADICEA.

WHEN the British warrior-queen,
    Bleeding from the Roman rods,
Sought with an indignant mien,
    Counsel of her country's gods;

Sage beneath the spreading oak
    Sat the Druid, hoary chief;
Every burning word he spoke,
    Full of rage and full of grief.

"Princess! if our aged eyes
    Weep upon thy matchless wrongs,
'Tis because resentment ties
    All the terrors of our tongues.

"Rome shall perish—write that word
    In the blood that she has spilt:
Perish, hopeless and abhorred,
    Deep in ruin as in guilt.

"Rome for empire far renowned,
    Tramples on a thousand states;
Soon her pride shall kiss the ground—
    Hark! the Gaul is at her gates!

TRANSLATIONS.   189

" Furens quid femina possit."

Quo secta virgis tempore Romulis,
Fastidiosa fronte, Britanniæ
 Regina bellatrix ad aras
  Indigetûm steterat deorum:

Quercu sedebat sub patula senex
Vates, nivali rex Druidûm coma;
 In carmen exarsurus ira
  Implacidum, implacidumque luctu.

" Natæne regum nil nisi lacrymam
Senes inanem reddimus, haud prius
 Vulgata perpessæ? Minaces
  Stringit enim dolor ipse linguas.

" Cadet—rubescant sanguine literæ,
Quem fudit, istæ—Roma; carens cadet
 Spe quaque, detestata terris;
  Mersa pari scelerum ruina.

" Late tyranno sub pede proterit
Jam mille gentes, ipsa tamen solo
 Æquanda. Nunc (adverte!) portas
  Gallus habet. Nova nequiores

"Other Romans shall arise,
  Heedless of a soldier's name;
Sounds, not arms, shall win the prize,
  Harmony the path to fame.

"Then the progeny that springs
  From the forests of our land,
Armed with thunder, clad with wings,
  Shall a wider world command.

"Regions Cæsar never knew
  Thy posterity shall sway;
Where his eagles never flew:
  None invincible as they."

Such the bard's prophetic words,
  Pregnant with celestial fire,
Bending as he swept the chords
  Of his sweet but awful lyre.

She, with all a monarch's pride,
  Felt them in her bosom glow;
Rushed to battle, fought and died;
  Dying hurled them at the foe.

" Ætas Quirites, pejor avis, feret,
Queis vile nomen militiæ; sonis,
   Non marte, quæsturos honorem;
     Voce viam reserante famæ.

"Exinde silvæ quam sobolem sinu
Gestant avitæ, fulmineis potens
   Pennis et alarum capesset
     Remigio populum ampliorem.

" Quas ipse nescit Cæsar, aheneus
Quas ales oras non adiit, tuos,
   Regina, fas torquere natos,
     Indocilem numerum repulsæ."

Hæc elocutus cælitus edito
Scatebat igni fatidicus senex:
   Dum, pronus in chordas, sonantem
     Dulce lyram modulatur iræ.

Queis illa sentit non humilis calens
Regina dictis: queis—ruerat nova
   In arma—bellatrix sub ipsum
     Funus adhuc premit acris hostes:—

"Ruffians, pitiless as proud,
  Heaven awards the vengeance due;
Empire is on us bestowed,
  Shame and ruin wait for you."

Cowper.

COME LIVE WITH ME.

COME, live with me, and be my love,
  And we will all the pleasures prove,
That valleys, groves, or hills, or field,
Or woods and steepy mountains yield.

And we will sit upon the rocks,
Seeing the shepherds feed their flocks
By shallow rivers, to whose falls
Melodious birds sing madrigals.

And I will make thee beds of roses
And a thousand fragrant posies:
A gown made of the finest wool,
Which from our pretty lambs we'll pull.

"At, durior grex omnibus, omnium
  Contemptor! æqui di quoque vindices
    Regnare nos optant : probrosa
      Vos perimi placitum ruina."

"*Et nos cedamus amori.*"

MOPSUS.

TRANSFER, amantis amans, laribus te, Lydia
    nostris—[1]
  Ruris uti cunctas experiamur opes :
Quot vallis, juga, saltus, ager, quot amœna ministret
    Mons gravis ascensu, quot vel amœna nemus.

Sæpius acclines saxo spectare juvarit
    Ducat uti pastum Thyrsis herile pecus ;
Sub vada rivorum, queis adsilientibus infra
    Concordes avibus suave loquantur aves.

Ipse rosas, queis fulta cubes caput, ipse recentum
    Quidquid alant florum pascua mille, feram :
Pro læna tibi vellus erit, neque tenuior usquam,
    Me socio teneras quo spoliaris oves.

[1] In the first edition this line stands as follows:—
MOPSUS.   Mopsi vive sodalis, ames age, Lydia, amantem!

The shepherd swains shall dance and sing
For thy delight each May morning:
If these delights thy mind may move,
Then live with me and be my love.

MARLOW.

IF all the world and love were young;
And truth in every shepherd's tongue,
These pretty pleasures might me move
To live with thee and be thy love.

Time drives the flocks from field to fold,
When rivers rage and rocks grow cold;
And Philomel becometh dumb,
The rest complain of cares to come.

But could youth last and love still breed,
Had joys no date nor age no need,
Then these delights my mind might move
To live with thee and be thy love.

RALEIGH.

Cantabunt salientque tibi pastoria pubes,
    Maia novum quoties jusserit ire diem:
Quæ si forte tibi sint oblectamina cordi,
    Vive comes Mopsi, Lydia, amantis amans.

Lydia.

FINGE nec huic mundo nec amoribus esse senectam;
    Pastorumque labris usque subesse fidem:
His forte illecebris (est his sua namque venustas)
    Mota, comes Mopsi viverem, amantis amans.

Tempus agit pecudes campis in ovile relictis;
    Fitque ferox fluvius frigidiusque jugum.
Dediscit Philomela modos et conticet ultro;
    Venturis querimur cætera turba malis.

Sin amor assidua subolesceret usque juventa,
    Nec joca cessarent, pluris egeret anus:
His equidem illecebris (est his sua namque venustas)
    Mota comes Mopsi viverem, amantis amans.

WHILE MUSING THUS.

WHILE musing thus, with contemplation fed
    And thousand fancies buzzing in my brain,
The sweet-tongued Philomel perched o'er my head,
And chanted forth a most melodious strain,
Which rapt me so with wonder and delight,
I judged my hearing better than my sight,
And wished me wings with her awhile to take my flight.

"O merry bird!" said I, "that fears no snares,
That neither toils, nor hoards up in thy barns,
Feels no sad thought, nor cruciating cares
To gain more good, or shun what might thee harm;
Thy clothes ne'er wear, thy meat is every where,
Thy bed a bough, thy drink the water clear,
Remind'st not what is past, nor what's to come dost fear."

"The dawning morn with songs thou dost prevent,
Set'st hundred notes unto thy feathered crew,

"*Avis in ramo tecta laremque parat.*"

STABAM multa movens, studio sic pastus inani,
  Somnia per vacuum dum fervent mille cerebrum:
Jamque canora mihi supra caput adstitit ales,
Et liquido Philomela modos e gutture fudit.
Obstupui; raptusque nova dulcedine dixi,
" Quanto oculis potior, quam traximus aure,
      voluptas."
Meque simul volui sumtis quatere æthera pennis.

" Fortunata nimis! Tibi retia nulla timori,
Te nullus labor urget, agis nec in horrea messes;
Nil conscire tibi, nulla tabescere culpa,
Sorte datum, quo plura petas, quo noxia vites.
At passim cibus, at sordent velamina nunquam:
Pocula sunt fontes liquidi tibi, fronsque cubile,
Nec memori veterum, nec mox ventura timenti.

Ante dies quam lucet ades, modulansque catervæ
Dividis aligeræ centum discrimina vocum.

So each one tunes his pretty instrument,
And warbling out the old, begins anew.
And thus they pass their youth in summer season,
Then follow thee into a better region,
Where winter's never felt by that sweet airy legion."

Anne Bradstreet.

SWEET DAY.

SWEET day, so cool, so calm, so bright,
    The bridal of the earth and sky:
The dew shall weep thy fall to-night;
        For thou must die.

Sweet rose, whose hue, angry and brave,
    Bids the rash gazer wipe his eye:
Thy root is ever in its grave;
        And thou must die.

Sweet Spring, full of sweet days and roses,
    A box where sweets compacted lie,
My music shows ye have your closes,
        And all must die.

Continuo ad cantum præludunt oribus illæ
Suavisonis; peragunt opus instaurantque peracta.
Hisque modis superante fovent æstate juventam.
Te duce dein abeunt in fortunatius arvum
Blanda volans legio, nulli penetrabile brumæ."

"*Parcent animæ fata superstiti.*"

LUX dulcis, cui tanta quies et frigus et ardor,
  Terræ polique nuptiæ,
At flebit tua fata tamen sub vesperis horam
  Ros, quippe leto debitæ.

Tuque, color cujus forti similisque minanti
  Temere tuentum lumina
Præstringit; radice lates tenus usque sepulchro;
  Et te perire fas, Rosa.

Dulces Maia refers hilaris lucesque rosasque,
  Thesaurus ingens dulcium.
Has sed in occasum me vergere disce magistro;
  Perire nam fas omnia.

> Only a sweet and virtuous soul,
>   Like seasoned timber, never gives;
> But though the whole world turn to coal,
>   Then chiefly lives.
>
> GEO. HERBERT.

IN MEMORIAM.

CVI.

THE time admits not flowers or leaves
   To deck the banquet. Fiercely flies
   The blast of North and East, and ice
Makes daggers at the sharpen'd eaves,

And bristles all the brakes and thorns
   To yon hard crescent, as she hangs
   Above the wood which grides and clangs
Its leafless ribs and iron horns

Together, in the drifts that pass,
   To darken on the rolling brine
   That breaks the coast. But fetch the wine,
Arrange the board and brim the glass;

Dulces ergo animæ demum et virtutis amantes
    Durant, ut ilex arida;
In fumum ac cinerem vertatur mundus: at illæ
    Tunc enitescent clarius.

In Memoriam.

NON hora myrto, non violis sinit
    Nitere mensas. Trux Aquilo foras
  Bacchatus inspicavit hastas
    E foribus glacies acutis;

Horretque saltus spinifer, algidæ
Sub falce lunæ; dum nemori imminet,
  Quod stridet illiditque costis
    Cornua, jam vacuis honorum,

Ferrata; nimbis prætereuntibus,
Ut incubent tandem implacido sali
  Qui curvat oras. Tu Falernum
    Prome, dapes strue, dic coronent

Bring in great logs and let them lie,
    To make a solid core of heat;
    Be cheerful-minded, talk and treat
Of all things ev'n as he were by:

We keep the day with festal cheer,
    With books and music. Surely we
    Will drink to him whate'er he be,
And sing the songs he loved to hear.

TENNYSON.

TEARS, IDLE TEARS.

TEARS, idle tears, I know not what they mean,
    Tears from the depth of some divine despair
Rise in the heart, and gather to the eyes,
In looking on the happy Autumn-fields,
And thinking of the days that are no more.

    Fresh as the first beam glittering on a sail,
That brings our friends up from the underworld,
Sad as the last which reddens over one
That sinks with all we love below the verge;
So sad, so fresh, the days that are no more.

Crateras: ignis cor solidum, graves
Repone ramos.   Jamque doloribus
  Loquare securus fugatis
    Quæ socio loquereris illo ;

Hunc dedicamus lætitiæ diem
Lyræque musisque.   Illius, illius
  Da, quicquid audit : nec silebunt
    Qui numeri placuere vivo.

Surgit amari aliquid.

SCILICET et lacrymas—quis dixerit unde profectas ?—
Nescio quod desiderium divinius imo
Nil profecturas e pectore cogit, et udi
Stant oculi : quoties auctumni aprica tuemur
Rura, diesque animo qui præteriere recursant.

  Dulce jubar, candent quo primo vela carinæ,
Altero ab orbe tuos tibi summittentis amicos :
Triste, quod in freta longa rubet condentibus isdem
Teque tuæque animæ partem.   Tam dulcis imago
Tam te tristis obit, qui præteriere, dierum.

Ah, sad and strange as in dark Summer dawns
The earliest pipe of half-awaken'd birds
To dying ears, when unto dying eyes
The casement slowly grows a glimmering square;
So sad, so strange, the days that are no more.

TENNYSON.

PSALM LV. v. 4.

MY heart is disquieted within me: and
The fear of death is fallen upon me.

Fearfulness and trembling are come upon me:
And an horrible dread hath overwhelmed me.

And I said, O that I had wings like a dove:
For then would I flee away, and be at rest.

Lo, then would I get me away far off;
And remain in the wilderness.

I would make haste to escape;
Because of the stormy wind and tempest.

Ægrum, ac tanquam aliunde, sonat morientis in
    aure
Excutientum avium sublustri mane sopores
Æstivus canor, incipiunt ubi languida circa
Lumina majores noto trepidare fenestræ.
Tanquam aliunde, dies qui præteriere revortunt.

"*Præsaga mali mens.*"

COR concitatum, quassaque senseram
   Instante leto pectora; senseram
    Terrore palescens, et artus
      Auguriis tremefactus atris:

Dixique tandem: "Verterer alitem
Nunc in columbam! scilicet in loca
    Longinqua deportarer, almæ
      Pacis amans; et inhospitales

Inter Gelonos, his fugiens procul
Terris, manerem.   Nulla fugam mora
    Tardaret, exosi procellæ
      Sævitiem, pluviosque ventos."

OF HOLIER JOY.

OF holier joy he sang, more true delight,
   In other happier isles for them reserved,
Who, faithful here, from constancy and right
   And truth have never swerved;

How evermore the tempered ocean-gales
   Breathe round those hidden islands of the blest,
Steeped in the glory spread, when day-light fails,
   Far in the sacred West.

How unto them, beyond our mortal night,
   Shines ever more in strength the golden day;
And meadows with purpureal roses bright
   Bloom round their feet alway;

And how 'twas given thro' virtue to aspire
   To golden seats in ever-calm abodes;
Of mortal men, admitted to the quire
   Of high immortal Gods.

TRENCH.

> "*Arva, beata
> Petamus arva.*"

TUM graviore canit vera oblectamina plectro,
    Beatiore queis in insula frui
Integros maneat vitæ; quæ fasque fidesque
    Diuque culta veritas det assequi.

Utque marina supra secretos usque piorum
    Agros susurret aura temperatius;
Agros, occidui saturet quos gloria Phœbi,
    Sacris in Occidentis ultimi locis.

Utque procul nobis, tenebris procul omnibus, illos
    Inauret usque vividus micans dies;
Purpureis distincta rosis ubi gleba perenni
    Nitore crura condat ambulantium.

Tanta dari castis. Utque affectetur ab isdem
    In aureis serena sedibus domus;
Mortalesque viros tandem immortalis in altum
    Receperit sedile numinum chorus.

FROM THE ANALOGY, Ch. I.

AND it is certain, that the bodies of all animals are in a constant flux, from that never-ceasing attrition which there is in every part of them. Now things of this kind unavoidably teach us to distinguish between these living agents ourselves, and large quantities of matter in which we are very nearly interested: since these may be alienated, and actually are in a daily course of succession, and changing their owners; while we are assured, that each living agent remains one and the same permanent being. And this general observation leads us to the following ones.

First; that we have no way of determining by experience what is the certain bulk of the living being each man calls himself: and yet, till it be determined that it is larger in bulk than the solid elementary particles of matter, which there is no ground to think any natural power can dissolve, there is no sort of reason to think death to be the dissolution of it, of the living being, even though it should not be absolutely indiscerptible. BUTLER.

"Non omnis moriar."

ID quoque constat, uti, quot corpora sunt animan-
    tum,
Non cessent fluere, assiduis quippe obvia plagis
Omni ex parte. Quibus monito distare fatendumst
Te qui vivis agisque, et molem materiai
Quantamvis, quacum sis nexus conque ligatus.
Has alienari quoniam vulgoque videmus
Trudi alias aliis, nec demum addicier ulli.
At, qui vivis agisque, manes certe unus et idem.
Queis animadversis audi quæ deinde sequantur.
    Principio, nunquam cognoveris experiundo
Mole sit id vivum quanta, quam quisque vocet se.
Quod tamen incerto sit majus mole minusve
Quam solida illa fuant corpuscula materiai,
(Quæ quis enim reputet natura posse resolvi?)
Nulla patet ratio cur solvi morte putaris
Hoc vivum, sit et hocce licet delebile tandem.

FOUNTAIN THAT SPARKLEST.

FOUNTAIN, that sparklest through the shady place,
Making a soft sad murmur o'er the stones
That strew thy lucid way! Oh, if some guest
Should haply wander near, with slow disease
Smitten, may thy cold springs the rose of health
Bring back, and the quick lustre to his eye!
The ancient oaks that on thy margin wave,
The song of birds, and through the rocky cave
The clear stream gushing, their according sounds
Should mingle, and like some strange music steal
Sadly, yet soothing, o'er his aching breast.
And thou pale exile from thy native shores
Here drink (O couldst thou! as of Lethe's stream!)
Nor friends, nor bleeding country, nor the views
Of hills or streams beloved, nor vesper's bell,
Heard in the twilight vale, remember more!

> "*juvat integros accedere fontes*
> *Atque haurire.*"

O QUI umbrosa micas inter loca, perque notantes
 Lucidum iter lapides, Fons, ita molle canis;
Molle quidem sed triste tamen:—si forte quis hospes
 Erret ad has, lenta tabe peractus, aquas;
Tu, precor, huic roseam gelido refer amne salutem,
 Inque oculo saliat, qualiter ante, nitor!
Scilicet antiquæ, riparum insignia, quercus,
 Puraque per durum quæ specus unda salit,
Voxque avium carmen poterunt sociare, quod illi
 Serpat ut insuetæ corda per ægra lyræ.
Sunt etenim mulcent quos tristia. Tuque paternis
 Qui procul ex oris pallidus exsul abes,
Hinc bibe—si posses Lethæum flumen! amici
 Nec tibi, nec moriens Roma sit ipsa moræ;
Non juga, non dulces fluvii, campana nec actum
 Sub ferruginea valle locuta diem.

FROM THE CHRISTIAN YEAR.

Go up and watch the new-born rill
    Just trickling from its mossy bed,
  Streaking the heath-clad hill
    With a bright emerald thread.

Canst thou her bold career foretell,
    What rocks she shall o'erleap or rend,
  How far in Ocean's swell
    Her freshening billows send?

Perchance that little brook shall flow
    The bulwark of some mighty realm,
  Bear navies to and fro
    With monarchs at their helm.

Or canst thou guess, how far away
    Some sister nymph, beside her urn
  Reclining night and day,
    'Mid reeds and mountain fern,

Nurses her store, with thine to blend
    When many a moor and glen are past,
  Then in the wide sea end
    Their spotless lives at last.

KEBLE.

"Parca metu primo."

I NUPER ortum suspice rivulum,
Vix e virenti qua trepidat toro,
   Clivumque vestitum genista
      Cærulei notat instar auri.

Dic quo feratur scilicet insolens?
Quæ scindet aut quæ transiliet juga?
   Quorsumve, dic, fluctus tumentem
      Mittet in Oceanum salubres?

Quem cernis est ut rivulus, imperi
Factus potentis præsidium, rates
   Hinc inde sit vecturus, ipsis
      Consulibus ratium magistris.

An scire fas est te, quibus in jugis
Acclinis urnæ nympha soror die
   Noctuque, montanaque tecta
      Carice arundineaque ripa,

Quodcunque apud se est pascat? At aviis
Elapsa silvis mox sociabitur
   Tecum, sub Ægæo patenti
      Innocuam positura vitam.

WINTER.

Low the woods
Bow their hoar head; and ere the languid sun
Faint from the west emits his evening ray,
Earth's universal face, deep hid and chill,
Is one wild dazzling waste, that buries wide
The works of man.   Drooping, the labourer-ox
Stands cover'd o'er with snow, and then demands
The fruit of all his toil.   The fowls of heaven,
Tamed by the cruel season, crowd around
The winnowing store, and claim the little boon
Which Providence assigns them.   One alone,
The redbreast, sacred to the household gods,
Wisely regardful of the embroiling sky,
In joyless fields and thorny thickets, leaves
His shivering mates, and pays to trusted man
His annual visit.   Half afraid, he first
Against the window beats; then, brisk, alights
On the warm hearth; then, hopping o'er the floor,
Eyes all the smiling family askance,
And pecks, and starts, and wonders where he is;
Till more familiar grown, the table crumbs
Attract his slender feet.   The foodless wilds
Pour forth their brown inhabitants.   The hare,

"*Aspera venit hiems.*"

CANA laborantes demittunt culmina silvæ.
Sol quoque languidior. Necdum jubar illius orto
Vespere ab Hesperiis trepidum se prodidit oris,
At tellus, quam magna, latet : stant frigore campi,
Ferales late campi candore maligno,
Obruiturque labos hominum. Stat taurus arator
Languida colla gravis multa nive : quid labor illum
Aut benefacta juvant? Domat inclementia cœli
Aerias volucres; vannumque frequenter Iacchi
Stipantes, quæ parva pater munuscula parvis
Donet habere Deus, poscunt. Deque omnibus una,
Rubro nota sinu, (propriam dixere Penates,)
Haud Jovis imprudens cœlum miscentis, in arvis
Illætabilibus et spinifero dumeto
Frigentes linquit socios, ac visit in annum
Tecta virum, fidens animi. Primumque fenestram
Spemque metumque inter, pulsat; mox acriter almum
Invasura focum. Dein interiora per aulæ
(Ridentes transversa tuens) it passibus æquis,
Quaque sit admirans, rostro petit et tremit alas.
Jamque levi pede, rebus ubi se assuevit, in ipsa
Frusta legit mensa. Furvum genus aspera mittunt
(Defit enim cibus) arva. Lepus, cui pectus inaudax,

Though timorous of heart, and hard beset
By death in various forms, dark snares and dogs,
And more unpitying men, the garden seeks,
Urged on by fearless want. The bleating kind
Eye the bleak heaven, and next the glistening earth,
With looks of dumb despair; then, sad dispersed,
Dig for the wither'd herbs through heaps of snow.
THOMSON.

"LEAVES HAVE THEIR TIME TO FALL."

LEAVES have their time to fall,
   And flowers to wither at the North-wind's
       breath,
And stars to set: but all,
   Thou hast all seasons for thine own, O Death!

Day is for mortal care,
   Eve for glad meetings at the joyous hearth,
Night for the dreams of sleep, the voice of prayer:
   But all for thee, thou mightiest of the earth!

The banquet has its hour,
   The feverish hour of mirth and song and wine:
There comes a day for grief's overwhelming shower,
   A time for softer tears: but all are thine.

Quam plaga quamque canes et plurima mortis imago,
Quamque premit cunctis homo durior, ipsa propinquat
(Vim dedit esuries) hortos.   Videt æthera tristem
Balantum pecus, arva videt splendentia, muto
Spem positam fassum obtutu.   Tum tristiter imo
E nive marcentes effossum spargitur herbas.

" Debemur morti nos nostraque."

FRONDES est ubi decidant,
    Marcescantque rosæ flatu Aquilonio:
  Horis astra cadunt suis;
Sed, Mors, cuncta tibi tempora vindicas.

  Curis nata virum dies;
Vesper colloquiis dulcibus ad focum;
    Somnis nox magis, et preci:
Sed nil, Terrigenum maxima, non tibi.

    Festis hora epulis datur,
(Fervens hora jocis, carminibus, mero;)
    Fusis altera lacrymis
Aut fletu tacito: quæque tamen tua.

Youth and the opening rose
  May look like things too glorious for decay,
And smile at thee!—but thou art not of those
  That wait the ripen'd bloom to seize their prey!

Felicia Hemans.

MY BROTHER.

My boyish days are nearly gone,
  My breast is not unsullied now;
And worldly cares and woes will soon
  Cut their deep furrows on my brow.

And life will take a darker hue
From ills my brother never knew:
And human passions o'er my soul
Now hold their dark and fell control:
And fear and envy, hate and rage,
Proclaim approaching manhood's age.

And I have made me bosom friends,
  And loved and linked my heart with others;
But who with mine his spirit blends
  As mine was blended with my brother's?

Virgo, seu rosa pullulans,
Tantum quippe nitent ut nequeant mori?
   Rident te? Neque enim soles
Prædæ parcere, dum flos adoleverit.

"*Ille meos, primum qui me sibi junxit, amores*
  Abstulit. Ille habeat secum servetque sepulcro."

PRÆTEREUNT nostræ, vel præteriere, juventæ
   Tempora; nec maculam nescit, ut ante, sinus.
Mox venient rerum curæ rerumque dolores;
   Et fronte in juveni ruga senilis erit.
Caligare mihi mox ipsa videbitur ætas,
   Tincta novis (frater nesciit illa) malis.
Nunc etiam quicunque viris solet esse libido
   Torva regunt animum truxque caterva meum:
Nunc livorque odiumque et mista timoribus ira
   Exagitant trepidum, Virque, loquuntur, eris.
Unanimos equidem legi coluique sodales;
   Fovi equidem multos interiore sinu:
Qua vero partem illam animæ, pars altera, quæram?
   Frater erat nostri pars ita, fratris ego.

When years of rapture glided by,
   The spring of life's unclouded weather,
Our souls were knit; and thou and I,
   My brother, grew in love together.
The chain is broke that bound us then.
When shall I find its like again?

MOULTRIE.

"LET US TURN HITHERWARD OUR BARK."

"Let us turn hitherward our bark," they cried,
   "And, 'mid the blisses of this happy isle,
Past toil forgetting and to come, abide
   In joyfulness awhile.

And then, refreshed, our tasks resume again,
   If other tasks we yet are bound unto,
Combing the hoary tresses of the main
   With sharp swift keel anew."

O heroes, that had once a nobler aim,
   O heroes, sprung from many a god-like line,
What will ye do, unmindful of your fame,
   And of your race divine?

Tunc, ubi felices labi non sensimus annos,
    Fulsit ubi verno sol sine nube polo;
Frater, erant nobis animi per mutua nexi;
    Par tibi tunc annis, par et amore fui.
Copula dissiluit qua nectebamur: at illi
    Dic quibus in latebris, qua sequar arte, parem?

Ὦ πέπονες, κάκ' ἐλέγχε', Ἀχαιΐδες, οὐκέτ' Ἀχαιοί.

"QUIN huc," fremebant, "dirigimus ratem:
    Hic, dote læti divitis insulæ,
      Paullisper hæremus, futuri
        Nec memores operis, nec acti:

"Curas refecti cras iterabimus,
Si qua supersunt emeritis novæ:
    Pexisse pernices acuta
      Canitiem pelagi carina."

O rebus olim nobilioribus
Pares: origo Dî quibus ac Deæ
    Heröes! oblitine famæ
      Hæc struitis, generisque summi?

But they, by these prevailing voices now
    Lured, evermore draw nearer to the land,
Nor saw the wrecks of many a goodly prow,
    That strewed that fatal strand;

Or seeing, feared not—warning taking none
    From the plain doom of all who went before,
Whose bones lay bleaching in the wind and sun,
    And whitened all the shore.

R. C. Trench.

ŒNONE.

O MOTHER, hear me yet before I die.
    Hear me, O earth. I will not die alone,
Lest their shrill happy laughter come to me
Walking the cold and starless road of Death
Uncomforted, leaving my ancient love
With the Greek woman. I will rise and go
Down into Troy, and ere the stars come forth
Talk with the wild Cassandra, for she says
A fire dances before her, and a sound
Rings ever in her ears of armed men.

Atqui propinquant jam magis ac magis,
Ducti magistra voce, solum : neque
   Videre prorarum nefandas
      Fragmina nobilium per oras;

Vidisse seu non pœnitet—ominis
Incuriosos tot præëuntium,
   Quorum ossa sol siccantque venti,
      Candet adhuc quibus omnis ora.

    "*longam incomitata videtur*
Ire viam."

QUAS moriens loquor, Ida parens, en accipe voces :
Accipe tu, tellus.   Non ibo sola sub umbras;
Fortunatorum risus ne verberet aurem,
Dum caligantes campos, jam frigida, Leti,
Jam nullo comitante, tero, priscumque maritum
Pellex Graia tenet.   Quin ibo ac Dorica castra
Deveniam : necdum surgentibus adloquar astris
Amentem Cassandram animi.   Nam lumina coram
Scintillare refert ignes, et murmur ad aurem
Tanquam armatorum nunquam cessare rotari.

What this may be I know not, but I know
That, wheresoe'er I am by night and day,
All earth and air seem only burning fire.

TENNYSON.

THE SOLDIER'S DREAM.

OUR bugles sang truce, for the night clouds had lowered,
    And the sentinel stars kept a watch in the sky;
And thousands had sunk on the ground overpowered,
    The weary to sleep and the wounded to die.

When reposing that night on my pallet of straw,
    By the wolf-scaring faggot that guarded the slain.
At the dead of the night a sweet vision I saw,
    And thrice ere the morning I dreamt it again.

Methought from the battlefield's dreadful array,
    Far, far I had roamed on a desolate track:
'Twas autumn—and sunshine arose on my way
    To the home of my father, that welcomed me back.

I flew to the pleasant fields traversed so oft
    In life's morning march, when my bosom was young;

Quæ quid monstra ferant, non auguror: id mihi
    demum
Nosse satis: quocunque feror noctuque dieque,
Igni stare mero tellusque videtur et aer.

" Cur hæc ego somnia vidi?"

NOX jam densa ruit: vigil undique sidus in æthra
    Excubat. Auditis ponimus arma tubis.
Mille peracta virum fluxerunt corpora campo,
    Occupet ut letum saucia, fessa sopor.

At mihi quem fultum custodit stramine parco
    Præsidium cæsis flamma lupisque metus,
Nocte super media dulcissima venit imago,
    Somniaque ante ortum ter rediere diem.

Arma feramque aciem mihi deseruisse videbar,
    Et desolatis longum iter ire viis.
Venerat auctumnus: desideriumque meorum
    Ad patrios ieram, sole favente, lares.

Quos jam in procinctu vitæ, jamque inscius ævi,
    Lustrabam toties, transferor ales agris:

I heard my own mountain-goats bleating aloft,
    And I knew the sweet strain that the corn-reapers
        sung.

Then pledged we the wine-cup, and fondly I swore
    From my home and my weeping friends never to
        part;
My little ones kissed me a thousand times o'er,
    And my wife sobbed aloud in her fulness of heart.

"Stay, stay with us—rest; thou art weary and
    worn;"
And fain was the war-broken soldier to stay:
But sorrow returned with the dawning of morn,
    And the voice in my dreaming ear melted away.
                            CAMPBELL.

THE BUTTERFLY.

AS rising on its purple wing
    The insect-queen of eastern spring,
O'er emerald meadows of Kashmeer
Invites the young pursuer near,
And leads him on from flower to flower
A weary chase and wasted hour,
Then leaves him, as it soars on high,

Audieram balare meas in rupe capellas;
　　Fallebat veteri carmine messor opus.

Sum quoque pollicitus, socia inter pocula, nunquam
　　Flentibus a sociis ire, meaque domo.
Oscula dant centum parvi, dein altera, nati :
　　Uxoris gremium rumpit anhelus amor :

" Fessus et æger ades, nobis ades usque," susurrat.
　　Fractus idem bellis miles et ipse volo.
Nequicquam.　Redeunte die rediere dolores.
　　Audieram voces : sed sopor illud erat.

" Neque enim levia aut ludicra petuntur."

PENNIS ut ostro tollitur æmulis
　　Quæ ver Eoüm papilio regit,
　Per gramen invitans smaragdo
　　Lucidius puerum sequacem ;
Vel has vel illas detinet ad rosas
Fessum vagandi, nec bene prodigum
　Horæ ; relinquens dein anhelo

With panting heart and tearful eye :
So Beauty lures the full-grown child,
With hue as bright, and wing as wild ;
A chase of idle hopes and fears,
Begun in folly, closed in tears,
If won, to equal ills betray'd,
Woe waits the insect and the maid ;
A life of pain, the loss of peace,
From infant's play and man's caprice :
The lovely toy so fiercely sought
Hath lost its charm by being caught,
For every touch that woo'd its stay
Hath brush'd its brightest hues away,
Till charm, and hue, and beauty gone
'Tis left to fly or fall alone.

BYRON.

GLENIFFER.

KEEN blaws the wind o'er the braes o' Gleniffer,
    The auld castle turrets are cover'd wi' snaw,
How changed frae the time when I met wi' my lover,
    Amang the broom bushes by Stanley green shaw.
The wild flowers o' simmer were spread a' sae bonnie,
    The mavis sang sweet frae the green birken tree ;

Ore, genis, abit ales, udis:
Per spes adultum sic puerum rapit
Metusque vanos, sic vario nitens
   Splendore, sic pennata, virgo;
     Cœpta miser flet inepta sero.
Vincas:—ad unum virgine prodita
Vermique fatum, par superest dolor
   Utrique; seu lascivus infans,
     Sive virum dederit libido
Vitam inquietam, ac mille gravem malis.
Sectamur acres dulcia: quæ simul
   Prensaris, amisere formam;
     Suasor enim digitus morarum
Sensim colores proterit aureos;
Donec recessit forma, color, venus:
   Te deinde securo, volarint
     Seu jaceant viduata campo.

" Versa loci facies."

RADIT Aricinæ vallis latus acriter aura,
   Nix grave longævis turribus hæret onus:
Non erat illa loci facies, ubi tecta genista
   Ad lucum viridem fabar, Amate veni.
Injussas jucunda rosas ibi pandidit æstas;
   Cantanti merulæ betula tegmen erat:

But far to the camp they ha'e march'd my dear
    Johnnie,
  And now it is winter wi' nature and me.

Then ilk thing around us was blythesome and
    cheerie,
  Then ilk thing around us was bonnie and braw :
Now naething is heard but the wind whistling
    drearie,
  And naething is seen but the wide-spreading snaw.
The trees are a' bare, and the birds mute and dowie,
  They shake the cauld drift frae their wings as they
    flee;
And chirp out their plaints, seeming wae for my
    Johnnie;
  'Tis winter wi' them and 'tis winter wi' me.

TANNAHILL.

HE sung what spirit thro' the whole mass is
    spread,
Everywhere all : how Heavens God's laws approve
And think it rest eternally to move :
How the kind Sun usefully comes and goes,
Wants it himself, yet gives to Man repose :
He sung how Earth blots the Moon's gilded wane

Nunc ad castra meus procul exsulat actus Amyntas :
　　Nunc eadem terris et mihi venit hiems.

Plurima lætitiæ tunc undique risit imago,
　　Cuique erat in gremio vis, et in ore nitor :
Nunc nihil audieris nisi mæsti sibila venti,
　　Nunc nihil aspicias hinc nisi et inde nivem.
Arbos muta ; silent pavefactæ, interque volandum
　　Excutiunt alis sessile frigus, aves ;
Voce loqui visæ blanda, Ploramus Amyntam.
　　Venit hiems illis : et mihi venit hiems.

"*Est Deus in nobis : agitante calescimus illo.*"

NAMQUE canebat uti, penetrans omnem undique, totam
Spiritus intus agat molem : confirmet ut æther
Jura Dei, requiemque putet sine fine moveri.
Sol ut eat redeatque suos iter almus in usus,
Detque viris, quanquam desideret ipse, soporem.
Aureaque ut lucem premat objice Cynthia terra,

Whilst foolish men beat sounding brass in vain,
Why the great waters her slight horns obey,
Her changing horns not constanter than they:
He sung how grisly comets hung in air,
Why swords and plagues attend their fatal hair,
God's beacons for the world, drawn up so far
To publish ills, and raise all earth to war:
What radiant pencil draws the watery bow,
What ties up hail, and picks the fleecy snow;
What palsy of the Earth here shakes fix'd hills
From off her brows, and here whole rivers spills.
Thus did this Heathen Nature's secrets tell,
And sometimes missed the cause, but sought it well.
COWLEY.

THE NEREIDS.

THE Nereid maids in days of yore
    Saw the lost pilot loose the helm,
Saw the wreck blacken all the shore,
    And every wave some head o'erwhelm.

Afar the youngest of the train
    Beheld (but fear'd and aided not)
A minstrel from the billowy main
    Borne breathless near her coral grot:

At stulti temere æra viri crepitantia plangant:
Unde regat parvis eadem mare cornubus ingens,
Queis mare non levius, non inconstantius, ipsum.
Cur visæ in cœlo tristes pendere cometæ,
Fatalemque comam morbique ensesque sequantur.
Illa deos dare signa viris, et figere cœlo,
Quo vulgent mala, quove vocent in prœlia gentes.
Quis radio pluvium describat gentibus arcum,
Vellera quid pectet nivis, ac tortum alliget imbrem.
Unde tremens tellus, nunc deturbarit in ipsa
Fronte sitos montes, nunc totum effuderit amnem.
Barbarus explicuit sic rerum arcana; latentes
Impar sæpe loqui, par semper quærere, causas.

"*Sedet æternumque sedebit.*"

NEREIDES (sic fama refert) videre puellæ
    Rector ut excideret puppe, subactus aquis:
Litus uti fractis nigresceret omne carinis,
    Omnis et abreptum volveret unda caput.
At procul a pelago stans una, novissima natu,
    (Ni metus obstaret, forte tulisset opem),
Semanimum vatem spumosis vidit ab undis
    Ad se—curalio tecta latebat—agi.

Then terror fled, and pity rose,
  "Ah me," she cried, "I come too late!
Rather than not have soothed his woes,
  I would, but may not, share his fate."

She raised his hand. "What hand like this
  Could reach the heart athwart the lyre?
What lips like these return my kiss,
  Or breathe, incessant, soft desire?"

From eve to morn, from morn to eve,
  She gazed his features o'er and o'er,
And those who love and who believe,
  May hear her sigh along the shore.
W. S. Landor.

WEEP NO MORE.

WEEP no more, nor sigh, nor groan;
  Sorrow calls no time that's gone;
Violets plucked, the sweetest rain
Makes not fresh nor grow again:
Trim thy locks, look cheerfully;
Fate's hidden ends eyes cannot see:
Joys as winged dreams fly fast;

Tum retro metus omnis iit, miserataque casum
    "Veni ego," conclamat, "væ mihi! sera nimis.
"Mallem equidem, tantos quam non mulsisse dolores,
    "Ipsa pari—possem si modo—sorte mori."

Inde levans dextram, "Num par," ait, "illius un-
    quam
    "Perveniet tacta cordis ad ima lyra?
"Talibus aut quisquam mihi dividet oscula labris,
    "Dum tenerum id numquam dicere cessat, Amo?"

Jamque dies nocti subit altera, noxque diei,
    At sedet, at vultum perlegit illa viri.
Illam, si quis amans et non incredulus idem est,
    Audiat ut circa litus anhelet adhuc.

"Ne doleas plus nimio."

FLENDI jam satis, et satis gemendi.
    Nec tempus lacrymis vocaris actum,
Carptis nec violis benigna quamvis
Nasci dat pluvia ac virere rursum.
Quin crines colis explicasque vultum?
Fati cæca nefas videre nobis.
Somni par fugit alitis voluptas:

Why should sadness longer last?
Grief is but a wound to woe;
Gentlest fair, mourn, mourn no mo.

       FLETCHER.

GLUMDALCLITCH'S LAMENT.

WHY did I trust thee with that giddy youth?
 Who from a page can ever learn the truth?
Versed in court-tricks, that money-loving boy
To some lord's daughter sold the living toy;
Or rent him limb from limb in cruel play,
As children tear the wings of flies away.
From place to place o'er Brobdingnag I'll roam,
And never will return, or bring thee home.
But who hath eyes to trace the passing wind?
How these thy fairy footsteps can I find?
Dost thou bewilder'd wander all alone
In the green thicket of a mossy stone;
Or, tumbled from the toadstool's slippery round,
Perhaps, all maim'd, lie grovelling on the ground?
Dost thou, embosom'd in the lovely rose,
Or sunk, within the peach's down, repose?
Within the kingcup if thy limbs are spread,
Or in the golden cowslip's velvet head,

Quidni tristitiæ modus sit idem ?
Fletu nil nisi prorogas dolorem.
Sat, dulcissima Philli, sat dolendi.

"*Illum absens absentem auditque videtque.*"

MENS levis est juvenum. Quid te commisimus illi ?
    Quisve putet famulo cuilibet esse fidem ?
Tene, ut Tulliolis esses ludibria vivus,
    Vendidit aularum doctus amansque lucri ?
Ceuve solent pueri pennas avellere muscis,
    Ossibus horribili distulit ossa joco ?
At Cyclopeas errabo hinc inde per oras :
    At referar nunquam, te nisi nacta, domum.
Sed quis enim celeres oculo deprenderit auras ?
    Qua Lemurum similes prosequar arte pedes ?
Muscosusne lapis, frondens te silva, fatigat,
    Quærentem socios exanimemque metu ?
An teretis nimium lapsus de vertice fungi,
    Cernuus incumbis membraque truncus humi ?
Purpureine lates tectus lanugine mali ?
    An rosa te gremio dulce soporat onus ?
Si calice in calthi totus jam extenderis, aut si
    Aureus in molli te vehit axe crocus :

O show me Flora, 'midst those sweets, the flower
Where sleeps my Grildrig in the fragrant bower?

But ah! I fear thy little fancy roves
On little females, and on little loves;
Thy pigmy children, and thy tiny spouse,
The baby playthings that adorn thy house,
Doors, windows, chimneys, and the spacious rooms,
Equal in size to cells of honeycombs:
Hast thou for these now ventured from the shore,
Thy bark a bean-shell and a straw thy oar?

POPE.

LAURA MATILDA'S DIRGE.

FROM "REJECTED ADDRESSES."

BALMY zephyrs, lightly flitting,
    Shade me with your azure wing;
On Parnassus' summit sitting,
    Aid me, Clio, while I sing.

Softly slept the dome of Drury
    O'er the empyreal crest,
When Alecto's sister-fury
    Softly slumb'ring sunk to rest.

Monstra, Flora, mihi, qui flos e millibus unus
    Silvula delicias condit odora meas!

Quanquam ah! quam vereor ne parvi forsan amores,
    Duxerit et parvum femina parva sinum.
Pigmæi pueri, veraque minutior uxor,
    Quotque tuos ornent frivola cunque lares:
Porta, fenestra, foci, spatiosæ scilicet aulæ,
    Mole pares cellis qua thyma condit apis;
Hæccine sunt litus pro queis abscondere nostrum
    Ausus eras, remo stramine, lintre faba?

Nænia.

O QUOT odoriferi volitatis in aëre venti,
    Cæruleum tegmen vestra sit ala mihi:
Tuque sedens Parnassus ubi caput erigit ingens,
    Dextra veni, Clio: teque docente canam.

Jam suaves somnos Tholus affectare Theatri
    Cæperat, igniflui trans laqueare poli:
Alectûs consanguineam quo tempore Erinnyn,
    Suave soporatam, cœpit adire quies.

Lo! from Lemnos limping lamely,
  Lags the lowly Lord of Fire,
Cytherea yielding tamely
  To the Cyclops dark and dire.

Clouds of amber, dreams of gladness,
  Dulcet joys and sports of youth,
Soon must yield to haughty sadness;
  Mercy holds the veil to Truth.

See Erostratus the second
  Fires again Diana's fane;
By the Fates from Orcus beckoned
  Clouds envelop Drury Lane.

Where is Cupid's crimson motion?
  Billowy ecstasy of woe,
Bear me straight, meandering ocean,
  Where the stagnant torrents flow.

Blood in every vein is gushing,
  Vixen vengeance lulls my heart;
See the Gorgon gang is rushing!
  Never, never let us part.

Lustra sed ecce labans claudo pede Lemnia linquit
   Luridus (at lente lugubriterque) Deus:
Amisit veteres, amisit inultus, amores;
   Teter habet Venerem terribilisque Cyclops.

Electri nebulas, potioraque somnia vero;
   Quotque placent pueris gaudia, quotque joci;
Omnia tristitiæ fas concessisse superbæ:
   Admissum Pietas scitque premitque nefas.

Respice! Nonne vides ut Erostratus alter ad ædem
   Rursus agat flammas, spreta Diana, tuam?
Mox, Acheronteis quas Parca eduxit ab antris,
   Druriacum nubes corripuere domum.

O ubi purpurei motus pueri alitis? o qui
   Me mihi turbineis surripis, angor, aquis!
Duc, labyrintheum, duc me, mare, tramite recto
   Quo rapidi fontes, pigra caterva, ruunt!

Jamque—soporat enim pectus Vindicta Virago;
   Omnibus a venis sanguinis unda salit;
Gorgoneique greges præceps (adverte!) feruntur—
   Sim, precor, o! semper sim tibi junctus ego.

HERRICK.   AMARILLIS.

HER.   MY dearest love, since thou wilt go,
      And leave me here behind thee;
For love or pitie, let me know
    The place where I may find thee.

AM.   In country meadowes, pearled with dew,
    And set about with lilies:
There, filling maunds with cowslips, you
    May find your Amarillis.

HER.   What have the meades to do with thee,
    Or with thy youthfull houres?
Live thee at court where thou may'st be
    The Queen of men, not flowers.

Let country wenches make 'em fine
    With posies, since 'tis fitter
For thee with richest jemmes to shine,
    And like the starres to glitter.

HERRICK.

In pratis studiosa florum.

HOR. O QUÆ sola places mihi,
    Si vis ire tamen, nosque relinquere,
  Dic te—si quis amor mei,
Si restat pietas—quo repetam loco?

AM. Inter pascua, ros ubi
    Par gemmæ rutilat, dædala liliis,
  Implentem calathos, tuam
Illic invenias fors Amaryllida.

HOR. Quid te pascua detinent
    Annis te teneris? I pete Cæsaris
  Aulam; non ibi flosculos
Flectes imperiis, sed potius viros.

  Certet rustica Phidyle
Se jactare rosis: te decorarier
  Gemmis rectius Indiæ
Et lucere parem sideris aurei.

CA' THE EWES.

As I gaed down the waterside,
    There I met my shepherd lad,
He row'd me sweetly in his plaid,
    And he ca'd me his dearie.

CHOR. Ca' the ewes to the knowes,
    Ca' them where the heather grows,
    Ca' them where the burnie flows,
        My bonnie dearie.

Will ye gang down the waterside,
And see the waves sae sweetly glide,
Beneath the hazels spreading wide?
    The moon it shines fu' clearly.

I was bred up at nae sic school,
My shepherd lad, to play the fool,
And a' the day to sit in dool,
    And naebody to see me.

Ye shall get gowns and ribbons meet,
Cauf-leather shoon upon your feet,
And in my arms ye's lie and sleep,
    And ye shall be my dearie.

Pastor, Virgo.

VIR. PASTOR erranti mihi propter amnem
　　Obvius venit meus, ambiensque
Suaviter palla, "Mihi," dixit, "una es,
　　Phylli, voluptas."

AMBO. Duc ad acclives tumulos, genista
　　Duc ubi frondent juga, rivulusque
Volvitur, matres gregis, o meorum
　　Finis amorum!

PAS. An libet ferri tibi propter amnem;
　　Cernere et fluctus, ut eant amœni
Subter umbrosas corylos, nec abdant
　　Nubila lunam?

VIR. Non erat primis mihi mos ab annis
　　Prosequi lusus, puer, inficetos;
Non queri, quam longa, diem, nec unquam
　　Cernier ulli.

PAS. Coaque, et vittæ tibi, quasque tergum
　　Det juvencorum soleæ ambulanti,
Dos erunt, nostris et onus lacertis
　　Dulce quiesces.

If ye'll but stand to what you've said,
I's gang wi' you, my shepherd lad,
And ye may rowe me in your plaid,
    And I sall be your dearie.

While waters wimple to the sea,
While day blinks in the lift sae hie,
Till clay-cauld death sall blind my eye
    Ye shall be my dearie.

BURNS.

THE GENTLE SHEPHERD.

PEG. O PATIE, let me gang, I mauna stay :
    We're baith cry'd hame, and Jeanie she's away.
PAT. I'm laith to part sae soon ; now we're alane,
    And Roger he's away wi' Jeanie gane :
    They're as content, for aught I hear or see,
    To be alane themselves, I judge, as we.
    Here, where primroses thickest paint the green,
    Hard by this little burnie let us lean :
    Hark ! how the lav'rocks chant aboon our heads,
    How saft the westlin' winds sough through the reeds.

vir. Hæreas istis modo rite dictis,
   Tum libens tecum, bone pastor, ibo;
   Pallium obduces mihi, meque dices
      Unus amatam.

pas. Dum patens amnes trepident in æquor,
   Rideat dum sol super arce cæli,
   Te, premet donec mea frigus orci
      Lumina, amabo.

Delia, Mopsus.

d. DECEDAM sine, Mopse; nefas mihi, Mopse, morari:
Phyllis abest, poscuntque domi me teque parentes.
m. Tam propere piget avelli; nunc denique nulli
   Cernimur, et Corydon cum Phyllide cessit in agros.
   Si qua fides oculis aut auribus, haud minus illis
Quam mihi quamque tibi solis, reor, esse voluntas.
Hic, narcissus ubi viridem densissimus agrum
Pingit, ad hunc tenuem flectamus corpora rivum.
Audis quem cantum supra det alauda, notique
Ut per arundineam suspirent leniter ulvam?

PEG. The scented meadow-birds and healthy breeze,
    For aught I ken, may mair than Peggy please.
PAT. Ye wrang me sair to doubt my being kind;
    In speaking sae, ye ca' me dull and blind,
    Gif I could fancy aught's sae sweet and fair
    As my sweet Meg, or worthy of my care.
    Thy breath is sweeter than the sweetest briar,
    Thy cheek and breast the finest flowers appear:
    Thy words excel the maist delightfu' notes
    That warble through the merle or mavis' throats:
    With thee I tent nae flowers that busk the field,
    Or ripest berries that our mountains yield;
    The sweetest fruits that hing upon the tree
    Are far inferior to a kiss of thee.
RAMSAY.

"POOR TREE."

POOR tree; a gentle mistress placed thee here,
    To be the glory of the glade around.
Thy life has not survived one fleeting year,
    And she too sleeps beneath another mound.

D. Suavis odor prati, volucresque auræque salubres,
   Credo equidem sunt, Mopse, magis quam Delia cordi.
M. Non equidem hoc merui : nostro diffidis amori ?
   Istud ais ?   Nimirum oculis et mente vacarem,
   Fingere si possem tam dulce et amabile quidquam,
   Tamve meæ dignum, quam dulcis Delia, curæ.
   Ora halant tua suave magis quocunque roseto ;
   Flos sinus, ac florum splendent par nobile malæ :
   At vox præcellit quod jucundissimum ab ullo
   Aut turdi aut merulæ stillatur gutture murmur.
   Me nulli alliciunt, pratorum insignia, flores,
   Bacca nec in clivis quamvis matura paternis,
   Sis modo tu mecum : prædulcia sustinet arbos
   Poma ; tamen pomis tua dulcius oscula Mopso.

Flebilis Arbor.

TE dominæ pia cura solo, miseranda, locarat
   Patentis, arbor, ut fores agri decus.
At mansit tua vita brevem non amplius annum ;
   At ipsa dormit extero sub aggere.

But mark what differing terms your fates allow,
  Though like the period of your swift decay ;
Thine are the sapless root and wither'd bough ;
  Hers the green memory and immortal day.

CARLISLE.

Quam diversa tamen sors est (adverte) duarum!
    Fugax utramque vexit hora; sed tibi,
Arbor, truncus iners, frons arida restat: at illi
    Perenne lumen ac virens adhuc amor.

Idem aliter redditum.

MOLLIS huc hera quam tulit caducam
    Ut saltus decus, arbor, emineres
Anno non superas brevi peracto;
    At cespes procul ambit arctus illam.
Pares funere (dispares eædem
    Quanto discite) marcuistis ambæ.
Frons restat tibi passa, sicca radix;
    Illi lux nova jugiter virenti.

*** *The six following translations were made for "Hymns Ancient and Modern, with some Metrical Translations," etc., published 1867.*

XLIV.—CHRISTMAS.

LANIGEROS, acclinis humo, pastoria pubes
    Custodiebat dum greges;
Splendescente polo longe lateque, Jehovæ
    Descendit ales nuncius.
Qui " Quid " ait " tremitis "—namque anxia pectora terror
    Immanis occupaverat—
" Grata fero: magnum jubeo lætarier et vos
    Et quicquid est mortalium.
Namque in Davidis urbe, satus quoque Davidis idem
    E stirpe, jamjam nascitur
Vestra Salus, Dominus vester, cognomine Christus;
    Signoque vobis hoc erit:
Invenietur ibi cælestis scilicet Infans,
    Spectabiturque jam viris;
Fascia velarit meritum non talia corpus,
    Condente præsepi caput."

Dixerat ales. Eo simul apparere videres
    Dicente lucentem chorum
Arce profectorum supera; pæanaque lætum
    His ordiebantur modis:
" Qui colit alta Deo summi tribuantur honores,
    Virisque pax arrideat;
Protenus excipiat cæli indulgentia terras,
    Haud dirimenda sæculis."

cxxx.—PENTECOST.

CAELO profecti vis et ira nuntiæ
    Fuere quondam Numinis:
Nimbos secantis pedibus; instar ignium
    Hac parte, nigros altera.
At prodeunti vis amorque denuo
    Ibant ministri; mollius
Sacer Palumbes dimovebat aera
    Quam mane primo flamina.
Quot occuparant impetu flammæ fero
    Arcem Sinai, suaviter
Tot consecratum nunc in omne defluunt
    Caput, corona nobilis.
Ac vox uti prægrandis arrectas metu,
    Ut clangor aures perculit,

(Cælestium quo cœtus audito tremunt,)
    E nocte trepidans nubium;
Sic prodeunte Spiritu Dei suos,
    Ut pastor, inventum greges,
Late sonabat vox, profecta cælitus,
    Tumultuosi turbinis.
Templum Jehovæ quâ, scatetque criminum
    Fecundus orbis undique;
In pervicaci scilicet demum sinu
    Desideratura locum.
Huc, Numen adsis! Vis, Amor, Prudentia,
    Adsis ut aures audiant;
Bene ominatum quisque captet ut diem
    Amore sospes an metu.

CXXXIX.

QUI pretium nostræ vitam dedit, ante 'Supremum
    Valete' quam vix edidit,
Solamenque Ducemque viris legarat eundem,
    Quo contubernales forent.
Venit at Ille suæ partem dulcedinis ultro
    Ut hospes efflaret bonus,
Nactus ubi semel esset, amat qua sede morari,
    Casti latebras pectoris.

Hinc illæ auditæ voces, qualemque susurrum
    Nascente captes Vespero;
Quo posuere metus, patitur quo frena libido,
    Spirare viso cælitus.
Ac virtutis inest si quid tibi, si quid honorum
    Claro triumphis contigit;
Venerit in mentem si quid divinius unquam;
    Hæc muneris sunt Illius.
At candens, at mite veni nunc, Numen, opemque
    Nostræ fer impotentiæ;
Cor nunc omne domus pateat tua; feceris omne
    Cor incola te dignius.
Vosque Patrem, Natum vos tollite; neve recuses
    Tu sancte laudem Spiritus:
Dignus enim tolli, Tria qui Deus audit in Uno,
    Unumve malit in Tribus.

CXCVII.

AUXILIUM quondam, nunc spes, Deus, unica nostri;
    Flante noto portus, præteritoque domus:
Gens habitat secura tuæ tua sedis in umbra;
    Simus ut incolumes efficit una manus.

Terræ olim neque forma fuit neque collibus ordo :
  Tu, quot eunt anni, numen es unus idem.
Sæcla vides abiisse, fugax ut vesper ; ut actis
  Quæ tenebris reducem prorogat hora diem.
*Stant populi, ceu mane novo juga florea, quorum
  Marcidus ad noctem falce jacebit honos :
*Tu "suboles terrena, redi" nec plura locuto,
  Quippe satæ gentes pulvere pulvis erunt.
Quos genuit, secum rotat usque volubilis ætas ;
  Ut sopor in cassum, luce solutus, eunt.
Tu quondam auxilium, spes nunc, Deus, ultima
    nostri,
  Sis columen trepidis, emeritisque domus.

---

  * Two stanzas are translated here which do not appear in the received editions of *Hymns Ancient and Modern.* They are quoted as part of this hymn by Miss Brontë in *Shirley,* and run as follows :

> "Thy word commands our flesh to dust—
>   'Return, ye sons of men ;'
> All nations rose from earth at first,
>   And turn to earth again.
>
> "Like flowery fields the nations stand,
>   Fresh in the morning light ;
> The flowers beneath the mower's hand
>   Lie withering ere 'tis night!"

Possibly Miss Brontë quoted from memory, and the true version of the first stanza may be—

> All nations rose from earth, and must
> Return to earth again.

CCXX.

QUO chaos ac tenebræ quondam fugere locuto,
    Supplicis, Omnipotens, accipe vota chori :
Quaque jubar nondum micuit quod sole, quod astris
    Clarius est, dicas " Exoriare dies ! "
Qui dignatus eras descendere more sequestri
    Alitis ad terram, luxque salusque virûm ;
Ægro mente salus, lux interioris egeno
    Luminis : at toto jam sit in orbe dies !
Unde fides, amor unde venit ; qui Spiritus audis ;
    Carpe, dator vitæ, sancte Palumbes, iter :
Incubet ætherios spargens tua forma nitores
    Fluctubus, ut terræ lustret opaca dies !
Quique, Triplex, splendes tamen integer ; ipse vicissim
    Robur, Amor, Virtus ; usque beate Deus :
Quale superbit aquis indignaturque teneri
    Fine carens pelagus, crescat ubique dies !

CCXLII.—DEDICATION OF A CHURCH.

VERBUM superni Numinis
    Qui cuncta comples, hanc domum
Amore certe consecres
Et feriatis annuas.
E fonte pueros hoc fluit
In criminosos gratia;
Beata cogit unctio
Nitere nuper sordidos.
Hic Christus animis dat cibo
Corpus suum fidelibus;
Cælestis agnus proprii
Fert ipse calycem sanguinis.
Hinc venia mœstis ac salus
Reis emenda; dum favet
Judex, et ingens gratia
Scelere sepultos integrat.
Hic, regnat alte qui Deus,
Benignus habitat; hic pium
Pectus gubernat atria
Desiderantum cælica
In dedicatam trux domum.'
Procella nequidquam furit;

Atrox eo vis Tartari
Passura fertur dedecus.
    At robur, at laus tibi, Pater,
    Sit comparique Filio;
    Diique amoris vinculo,
    Dum sæcla currunt, Flamini.

www.ingramcontent.com/pod-product-compliance
Lightning Source LLC
Chambersburg PA
CBHW032139230426
43672CB00011B/2388